Elizabethan Demonology

by Thomas Alfred Spalding

1880

TO

ROBERT BROWNING,

PRESIDENT OF THE

NEW SHAKSPERE SOCIETY,

THIS VOLUME IS DEDICATED.

FOREWORD.

This Essay is an expansion, in accordance with a preconceived scheme, of two papers, one on "The Witches in Macbeth," and the other on "The Demonology of Shakspere," which were read before the New Shakspere Society in the years 1877 and 1878. The Shakspere references in the text are made to the Globe Edition.

The writer's best thanks are due to his friends Mr. F.J. Furnivall and Mr. Lauriston E. Shaw, for their kindness in reading the proof sheets, and suggesting emendations.

TEMPLE,

October 7, 1879.

"We are too hasty when we set down our ancestors in the gross for fools for the monstrous inconsistencies (as they seem to us) involved in their creed of witchcraft."—C. LAMB.

"But I will say, of Shakspere's works generally, that we have no full impress of him there, even as full as we have of many men. His works are so many windows, through which we see a glimpse of the world that was in him."—T. CARLYLE.

ANALYSIS.

I.

1. Difficulty in understanding our elder writers without a knowledge of their language and ideas. 2. Especially in the case of dramatic poets. 3. Examples.

Hamlet's "assume a virtue." 4. Changes in ideas and law relating to marriage.

Massinger's "Maid of Honour" as an example. 5. *Sponsalia de futuro* and *Sponsalia de praesenti*. Shakspere's marriage. 6. Student's duty is to get to know the opinions and feelings of the folk amongst whom his author lived. 7. It will be hard work, but a gain in the end. First, in preventing conceit. 8. Secondly, in preventing rambling reading. 9. Author's present object to illustrate the dead belief in Demonology, especially as far as it concerns Shakspere. He thinks that this may perhaps bring us into closer contact with Shakspere's soul. 10. Some one objects that Shakspere can speak better for himself. Yes, but we must be sure that we understand the media through which he speaks. 11. Division of subject.

II.

12. Reasons why the empire of the supernatural is so extended amongst savages.

13. All important affairs of life transacted under superintendence of Supreme Powers. 14. What are these Powers? Three principles regarding them. 15. (I.) Incapacity of mankind to accept monotheism. The Jews. 16. Roman Catholicism really polytheistic, although believers won't admit it. Virgin Mary. Saints.

Angels. Protestantism in the same condition in a less degree. 17. Francis of Assisi. Gradually made into a god. 18. (II.) Manichaeism. Evil spirits as inevitable as good. 19. (III.) Tendency to treat the gods of hostile religions as devils. 20. In the Greek theology. [Greek: daimones]. Platonism. 21. Neo-Platonism. Makes the elder gods into daemons. 22. Judaism. Recognizes foreign gods at first. *Elohim*, but they get degraded in time. Beelzebub, Belial, etc. 23.

Early Christians treat gods of Greece in the same way. St. Paul's view. 24. The Church, however, did not stick to its colours in this respect. Honesty not the best

policy. A policy of compromise. 25. The oracles. Sosthenion and

3

St. Michael.

Delphi. St. Gregory's saintliness and magnanimity. Confusion of pagan gods and Christian saints. 26. Church in North Europe. Thonar, etc., are devils, but Balda gets identified with Christ. 27. Conversion of Britons. Their gods get turned into fairies rather than devils. Deuce. Old Nick. 28. Subsequent evolution of belief.

Carlyle's Abbot Sampson. Religious formulae of witchcraft. 29. The Reformers and Catholics revive the old accusations. The Reformers only go half-way in scepticism. Calfhill and Martiall. 30. Catholics. Siege of Alkmaar. Unfortunate mistake of a Spanish prisoner. 31. Conditions that tended to vivify the belief during Elizabethan era. 32. The new freedom. Want of rules of evidence. Arthur Hacket and his madnesses. Sneezing. Cock-crowing. Jackdaw in the House of Commons. Russell and Drake both mistaken for devils. 33. Credulousness of people. "To make one danse naked." A parson's proof of transubstantiation. 34.

But the Elizabethans had strong common sense nevertheless. People do wrong if they set them down as fools. If we had not learned to be wiser than they, we should have to be ashamed of ourselves. We shall learn nothing from them if we don't try to understand them.

III.

35. The three heads. 36. (I.) Classification of devils. Greater and lesser devils.

Good and bad angels. 37. Another classification, not popular. 38. Names of greater devils. Horribly uncouth. The number of them. Shakspere's devils. 39.

(II.) Form of devils of the greater. 40. Of the lesser. The horns, goggle eyes, and tail. Scot's carnal-mindedness. He gets his book burnt, and written against by James I. 41. Spenser's idol-devil. 42. Dramatists' satire of popular opinion. 43.

Favourite form for appearing in when conjured. Devils in Macbeth. 44. Powers of devils. 45. Catholic belief in devil's power to create bodies. 46. Reformers deny this, but admit that he deceives people into believing that he can do so, either by getting hold of a dead body, and restoring animation. 47. Or by means of illusion. 48. The common people stuck to the Catholic doctrine. Devils appear in likeness of an ordinary human being. 49. Even a living one, which was sometimes awkward. "The Troublesome Raigne of King John." They like to appear as priests or parsons. The devil quoting Scripture. 50. Other human shapes. 51. Animals. Ariel. 52. Puck. 53. "The Witch of Edmonton." The devil on the stage. Flies. Urban Grandier. Sir M. Hale. 54. Devils as angels. As Christ.

55. As dead friend. Reformers denied the possibility of ghosts, and said the appearances so called were devils. James I. and his opinion. 56. The common people believed in the ghosts. Bishop Pilkington's troubles. 57. The two theories.

Illustrated in "Julius Caesar,""Macbeth." 58. And "Hamlet." 59. This explains an apparent inconsistency in "Hamlet." 60. Possession and obsession. Again the Catholics and Protestants differ. 61. But the common people believe in possession. 62. Ignorance on the subject of mental disease. The exorcists. 63.

John Cotta on possession. What the "learned physicion" knew. 64. What was manifest to the vulgar view. Will Sommers. "The Devil is an Ass." 65. Harsnet's

"Declaration," and "King Lear." 66. The Babington conspiracy. 67. Weston, alias Edmonds. His exorcisms. Mainy. The basis of Harsnet's statements. 69. The devils in "Lear." 70. Edgar and Mainy. Mainy's loose morals. 71. The devils tempt with knives and halters. 72. Mainy's seven devils: Pride, Covetousness, Luxury, Envy, Wrath, Gluttony, Sloth. The Nightingale business. 73. Treatment of the possessed: confinement, flagellation. 74. Dr Pinch. Nicknames. 75. Other methods. That of "Elias and Pawle". The holy chair, sack and oil, brimstone. 76.

Firing out. 77. Bodily diseases the work of the devil. Bishop Hooper on hygiene.

78. But devils couldn't kill people unless they renounced God. 79. Witchcraft.

80. People now-a-days can't sympathize with the witch persecutors, because they don't believe in the devil. Satan is a mere theory now. 81. But they believed in him once, and therefore killed people that were suspected of having to do with him. 82. And we don't sympathize with the persecuted witches, although we make a great fuss about the sufferings of the Reformers. 83. The witches in Macbeth. Some take them to be Norns. 84. Gervinus. His opinion. 85. Mr. F.G.

Fleay. His opinion. 86. Evidence. Simon Forman's note. 87. Holinshed's account.

88. Criticism. 89. It is said that the appearance and powers of the sisters are not those of witches. 90. It is going to be shown that they are. 91. A third piece of criticism. 92. Objections. 93. Contemporary descriptions of witches. Scot, Harsnet. Witches' beards. 94. Have Norns chappy fingers, skinny lips, and beards? 95. Powers of witches "looking into the seeds of time." Bessie Roy, how she looked into them. 96. Meaning of first scene of "Macbeth." 97. Witches power to vanish. Ointments for the purpose. Scot's instance of their efficacy. 98.

"Weird sisters." 99. Other evidence. 100. Why Shakspere chose witches.

Command over elements. 101. Peculiar to Scotch trials of 1590-91. 102. Earlier case of Bessie Dunlop—a poor, starved, half daft creature. "Thom Reid," and how he tempted her. Her canny Scotch prudence. Poor Bessie gets burnt for all that. 103. Reason for peculiarity of trials of 1590. James II. comes from Denmark to Scotland. The witches raise a storm at the instigation of the devil.

How the trials were conducted. 104. John Fian. Raising a mist. Toad-omen. Ship sinking. 105. Sieve-sailing. Excitement south of the Border. The

"Daemonologie." Statute of James against witchcraft. 106. The origin of the incubus and succubus. 107. Mooncalves. 108. Division of opinion amongst

Reformers regarding devils. Giordano Bruno. Bullinger's opinion about Sadducees and Epicures. 109. Emancipation a gradual process. Exorcism in Edward VI.'s Prayer-book. 110. The author hopes he has been reverent in his treatment of the subject. Any sincere belief entitled to respect. Our pet beliefs may some day appear as dead and ridiculous as these.

IV.

111. Fairies and devils differ in degree, not in origin. 112. Evidence. 113. Cause of difference. Folk, until disturbed by religious doubt, don't believe in devils, but fairies. 114. Reformation shook people up, and made them think of hell and devils. 115. The change came in the towns before the country. Fairies held on a long time in the country. 116. Shakspere was early impressed with fairy lore. In middle life, came in contact with town thought and devils, and at the end of it returned to Stratford and fairydom. 117. This is reflected in his works. 118. But there is progression of thought to be observed in these stages. 119. Shakspere indirectly tells us his thoughts, if we will take the trouble to learn them. 120.

Three stages of thought that men go through on religious matters. Hereditary belief. Scepticism. Reasoned belief. 121. Shakspere went through all this. 122.

Illustrations. Hereditary belief. "A Midsummer Night's Dream." Fairies chiefly an adaptation of current tradition. 123. The dawn of doubt. 124. Scepticism. Evil spirits dominant. No guiding good. 125.

Corresponding lapse of faith in other matters. Woman's purity. 126. Man's honour. 127. Mr. Ruskin's view of Shakspere's message. 128. Founded chiefly on plays of sceptical period.

Message of third period entirely different. 129. Reasoned belief. "The Tempest."

130. Man can master evil of all forms if he go about it in the right way—is not the toy of fate. 131. Prospero a type of Shakspere in this final stage of thought.

How pleasant to think this!

ELIZABETHAN DEMONOLOGY.

1. It is impossible to understand and appreciate thoroughly the production of any great literary genius who lived and wrote in times far removed from our own, without a certain amount of familiarity, not only with the precise shades of meaning possessed by the vocabulary he made use of, as distinguished from the sense conveyed by the same words in the present day, but also with the customs and ideas, political, religious and moral, that predominated during the period in which his works were produced. Without such information, it will be found impossible, in many matters of the first importance, to grasp the writer's true intent, and much will appear vague and lifeless that was full of point and vigour when it was first conceived; or, worse still, modern opinion upon the subject will be set up as the standard of interpretation, ideas will be forced into the writer's sentences that could not by any manner of possibility have had place in his mind, and utterly false conclusions as to his meaning will be the result. Even the man who has had some experience in the study of an early literature, occasionally finds some difficulty in preventing the current opinions of his day from obtruding themselves upon his work and warping his judgment; to the general reader this must indeed be a frequent and serious stumbling-block.

2. This is a special source of danger in the study of the works of

dramatic poets, whose very art lies in the representation of the current opinions, habits, and foibles of their times—in holding up the mirror to their age. It is true that, if their works are to live, they must deal with subjects of more than mere passing interest; but it is also true that many, and the greatest of them, speak upon questions of eternal interest in the particular light cast upon them in their times, and it is quite possible that the truth may be entirely lost from want of power to recognize it under the disguise in which it comes. A certain motive, for instance, that is an overpowering one in a given period, subsequently appears grotesque, weak, or even powerless; the consequent action becomes incomprehensible, and the actor is contemned; and a simile that appeared most appropriate in the ears of the author's contemporaries, seems meaningless, or ridiculous, to later generations.

3. An example or two of this possibility of error, derived from works produced during the period with which it is the object of these pages to deal, will not be out of place here.

A very striking illustration of the manner in which a word may mislead is afforded by the oft-quoted line:

"Assume a virtue, if you have it not."

By most readers the secondary, and, in the present day, almost universal, meaning of the word assume—"pretend that to be, which in reality has no existence;"—that is, in the particular case, "ape the chastity you do not in reality possess"—is understood in this sentence; and consequently Hamlet, and through him, Shakspere, stand committed to the appalling doctrine that hypocrisy in morals is to be commended and cultivated. Now, such a proposition never for an instant entered Shakspere's head. He used the word "assume" in this case in its primary and justest sense; *ad-sumo*, take to, acquire; and the context plainly shows that Hamlet meant that his mother, by self-denial, would gradually acquire that virtue in which she was so conspicuously wanting. Yet, for lack of a little knowledge of the history of the word employed, the other monstrous gloss has received almost universal and applauding acceptance.

4. This is a fair example of the style of error which a reader unacquainted with the history of the changes our language has undergone may fall into. Ignorance of changes in customs and morals may cause equal or greater error.

The difference between the older and more modern law, and popular opinion, relating to promises of marriage and their fulfilment, affords a striking illustration of the absurdities that attend upon the interpretation of the ideas of one generation by the practice of another. Perhaps no greater nonsense has been talked upon any subject than this one, especially in relation to Shakspere's own marriage, by critics who seem to have thought that a fervent expression of acute moral feeling would replace and render unnecessary patient investigation.

In illustration of this difference, a play of Massinger's, "The Maid of Honour," may be advantageously cited, as the catastrophe turns upon this question of marriage contracts. Camiola, the heroine, having been precontracted by oath[1]

to Bertoldo, the king's natural brother, and hearing of his subsequent engagement to the Duchess of Sienna, determines to quit the world and take the veil. But before doing so, and without informing any one, except her confessor, of her intention, she contrives a somewhat dramatic scene for the purpose of exposing her false lover. She comes into the presence of the king and all the court, produces her contract, claims Bertoldo as her husband, and demands justice of the king, adjuring him that he shall not—

"Swayed or by favour or affection,

By a false gloss or wrested comment, alter

The true intent and letter of the law."

[Footnote 1: Act v. sc. I.]

Now, the only remedy that would occur to the mind of the reader of the present day under such circumstances, would be an action for breach of promise of marriage, and he would probably be aware of the very recent origin of that method of procedure. The only reply, therefore, that he would expect from Roberto would be a mild and sympathetic assurance of inability to interfere; and he must be somewhat taken aback to find this claim of Camiola admitted as indisputable. The riddle becomes somewhat further involved when, having established her contract, she immediately intimates that she has not the slightest intention of observing it herself, by declaring her desire to take the veil.

5. This can only be explained by the rules current at the time regarding spousals.

The betrothal, or handfasting, was, in Massinger's time, a ceremony that entailed very serious obligations upon the parties to it. There were two classes of spousals— *sponsalia de futuro* and *sponsalia de praesenti*: a promise of marriage in the future, and an actual declaration of present marriage. This last form of betrothal was, in fact, marriage, as far as the contracting parties were concerned.

[1] It could not, even though not consummated, be dissolved by mutual consent; and a subsequent marriage, even though celebrated with religious rites, was utterly invalid, and could be set aside at the suit of the injured person.

[Footnote 1: Swinburne, A Treatise of Spousals, 1686, p. 236. In England the offspring were, nevertheless, illegitimate.]

The results entailed by *sponsalia de futuro* were less serious. Although no spousals of the same nature could be entered into with a third person during the

existence of the contract, yet it could be dissolved by mutual consent, and was dissolved by subsequent *sponsalia in praesenti*, or matrimony. But such spousals could be converted into valid matrimony by the cohabitation of the parties; and this, instead of being looked upon as reprehensible, seems to have been treated as a laudable action, and to be by all means encouraged.[1] In addition to this, completion of a contract for marriage *de futuro* confirmed by oath, if such a contract were not indeed indissoluble, as was thought by some, could at any rate be enforced against an unwilling party. But there were some reasons that justified the dissolution of *sponsalia* of either description. Affinity was one of these; and—what is to the purpose here, in England before the Reformation, and in those parts of the continent unaffected by it—the entrance into a religious order was another. Here, then, we have a full explanation of Camiola's conduct.

She is in possession of evidence of a contract of marriage between herself and Bertoldo, which, whether *in praesenti* or *in futuro*, being confirmed by oath, she can force upon him, and which will invalidate his proposed marriage with the duchess. Having established her right, she takes the only step that can with certainty free both herself and Bertoldo from the bond they had created, by retiring into a nunnery.

[Footnote 1: Swinburne, p. 227.]

This explanation renders the action of the play clear, and at the same time shows that Shakspere in his conduct with regard to his marriage may have been behaving in the most honourable and praiseworthy manner; as the bond, with the date of which the date of the birth of his first child is compared, is for the purpose of exonerating the ecclesiastics from any liability for performing the ecclesiastical ceremony, which was not at all a necessary preliminary to a valid marriage, so far as the husband and wife were concerned, although it was essential to render issue of the marriage legitimate.

6. These are instances of the deceptions that are likely to arise from the two fertile sources that have been specified. There can be no doubt that the existence of errors arising from the former source—

misapprehension of the meaning of words—is very generally admitted, and effectual remedies have been supplied by modern scholars for those who will make use of them. Errors arising from the latter source are not so entirely recognized, or so securely guarded against. But what has just been said surely shows that it is of no use reading a writer of a past age with merely modern conceptions; and, therefore, that if such a man's works are worth study at all, they must be read with the help of the light thrown uponthem by contemporary history, literature, laws, and morals. The student must endeavour to divest himself, as far as possible, of all ideas that are the result of a development subsequent to the time in which his author lived, and to place himself in harmony with the life and thoughts of the people of that age: sit down with them in their homes, and learn the sources of their loves, their hates, their fears, and see wherein domestic happiness, or lack of it, made them strong or weak; follow them to the market-place, and witness their dealings with their fellows—the honesty or baseness of them, and trace the cause; look into their very hearts, if it may be, as they kneel at the devotion they feel or simulate, and become acquainted with the springs of their dearest aspirations and most secret prayers.

7. A hard discipline, no doubt, but not more hard than salutary. Salutary in two ways. First, as a test of the student's own earnestness of purpose. For in these days of revival of interest in our elder literature, it has become much the custom for flippant persons, who are covetous of being thought "well-read" by their less-enterprising companions, to skim over the surface of the pages of the wisest and noblest of our great teachers, either not understanding, or misunderstanding them. "I have read Chaucer, Shakspere, Milton," is the sublimely satirical expression constantly heard from the mouths of those who, having read words set down by the men they name, have no more capacity for reading the hearts of the men themselves, through those words, than a blind man has for discerning the colour of flowers. As a consequence of this flippancy of reading, numberless writers, whose works have long been consigned to a well-merited oblivion, have of late years been disinterred and held up for public admiration, chiefly upon the ground that they are ancient and unknown. The man who reads for the sake of having done so, not for the sake of the knowledge gained by doing so, finds as much charm in these

petty writers as in the greater, and hence their transient and undeserved popularity. It would be well, then, for every earnest student, before beginning the study of any one having pretensions to the position of a master, and who is not of our own generation, to ask himself, "Am I prepared thoroughly to sift out and ascertain the true import of every allusion contained in this volume?" And if he cannot honestly answer "Yes," let him shut the book, assured that he is not impelled to the study of it by a sincere thirst for knowledge, but by impertinent curiosity, or a shallow desire to obtain undeserved credit for learning.

8. The second way in which such a discipline will prove salutary is this: it will prevent the student from straying too far afield in his reading. The number of

"classical" authors whose works will repay such severe study is extremely limited. However much enthusiasm he may throw into his studies, he will find that nine-tenths of our older literature yields too small a harvest of instruction to attract any but the pedant to expend so much labour upon them. The two great vices of modern reading will be avoided—flippancy on the one hand, and pedantry on the other.

9. The object, therefore, which I have had in view in the compilation of the following pages, is to attempt to throw some additional light upon a condition of thought, utterly different from any belief that has firm hold in the present generation, that was current and peculiarly prominent during the lifetime of the man who bears overwhelmingly the greatest name, either in our own or any other literature. It may be said, and perhaps with much force, that enough, and more than enough, has been written in the way of Shakspere criticism. But is it not better that somewhat too much should be written upon such a subject than too little? We cannot expect that every one shall see all the greatness of Shakspere's vast and complex mind—by one a truth will be grasped that has eluded the vigilance of others;—and it is better that those who can by no possibility grasp anything at all should have patient hearing, rather than that any additional light should be lost. The useless, lifeless criticism vanishes quietly away into chaos; the good remains

quietly to be useful: and it is in reliance upon the justice and certainty of this law that I aim at bringing before the mind, as clearly as may be, a phase of belief that was continually and powerfully influencing Shakspere during the whole of his life, but is now well-nigh forgotten or entirely misunderstood. If the endeavour is a useless and unprofitable one, let it be forgotten—I am content; but I hope to be able to show that an investigation of the subject does furnish us with a key which, in a manner, unlocks the secrets of Shakspere's heart, and brings us closer to the real living man—to the very soul of him who, with hardly any history in the accepted sense of the word, has left us in his works a biography of far deeper and more precious meaning, if we will but understand it.

10. But it may be said that Shakspere, of all men, is able to speak for himself without aid or comment. His works appeal to all, young and old, in every time, every nation. It is true; he can be understood. He is, to use again Ben Jonson's oft-quoted words, "Not of an age, but for all time." Yet he is so thoroughly imbued with the spirit and opinions of his era, that without a certain comprehension of the men of the Elizabethan period he cannot be understood fully. Indeed, his greatness is to a large extent due to his sympathy with the menaround him, his power of clearly thinking out the answers to the all-time questions, and giving a voice to them that his contemporaries could understand; —answers that others could not for themselves formulate—could, perhaps, only vaguely and dimly feel after. To understand these answers fully, the language in which they were delivered must be first thoroughly mastered.

11. I intend, therefore, to attempt to sketch out the leading features of a phase of religious belief that acquired peculiar distinctness and prominence during Shakspere's lifetime—more, perhaps, than it ever did before, or has done since—

the belief in the existence of evil spirits, and their influence upon and dealings with mankind. The subject will be treated in three sections. The first will contain a short statement of the laws that seem to be of universal operation in the creation and maintenance of the belief in a multitudinous band of spirits, good and evil; and of a few of the conditions of the Elizabethan epoch that may have had a formative and modifying influence upon that belief. The second will be devoted to an outline of the chief features of that belief, as it existed at the time in question—the organization, appearance, and various functions and powers of the evil spirits, with special reference to Shakspere's plays. The third and concluding section, will embody an attempt to trace the growth of Shakspere's thought upon religious matters through the medium of his allusions to this subject.

* * * * *

12. The empire of the supernatural must obviously be most extended where civilization is the least advanced. An educated man has to make a conscious, and sometimes severe, effort to refrain from pronouncing a dogmatic opinion as to the cause of a given result when sufficient evidence to warrant a definite conclusion is wanting; to the savage, the notion of any necessity for, or advantage to be derived from, such self-restraint never once occurs. Neither the lightning that strikes his hut, the blight that withers his crops, the disease that destroys the life of those he loves; nor, on the other hand, the beneficent sunshine or life-giving rain, is by him traceable to any known physical cause.

They are the results of influences utterly beyond his understanding—supernatural,—matters upon which imagination is allowed free scope to run riot, and from which spring up a legion of myths, or attempts to represent in some manner these incomprehensible processes, grotesque or poetic, according to the character of the people with which they originate, which, if their growth be not disturbed by extraneous influences, eventually develop into the national creed.

The most ordinary events of the savage's every-day life do not admit of a natural solution; his whole existence is bound in, from birth to death, by a network of miracles, and regulated, in its smallest details, by unseen powers of whom he knows little or nothing.

13. Hence it is that, in primitive societies, the functions of

legislator, judge, priest, and medicine man are all combined in one individual, the great medium of communication between man and the unknown, whose person is pre-eminently sacred. The laws that are to guide the community come in some mysterious manner through him from the higher powers. If two members of the clan are involved in a quarrel, he is appealed to to apply some test in order to ascertain which of the two is in the wrong—an ordeal that can have no judicial operation, except upon the assumption of the existence of omnipotent beings interested in the discovery of evil-doers, who will prevent the test from operating unjustly. Maladies and famines are unmistakeable signs of the displeasure of the good, or spite of the bad spirits, and are to be averted by some propitiatory act on the part of the sufferers, or the mediation of the priest-doctor. The remedy that would put an end to a long-continued drought will be equally effective in arresting an epidemic.

14. But who, and of what nature, are these supernatural powers whose influences are thus brought to bear upon every-day life, and who appear to take such an interest in the affairs of mankind? It seems that there are three great principles at work in the evolution and modification of the ideas upon this subject, which must now be shortly stated.

15. (i.) The first of these is the apparent incapacity of the majority of mankind to accept a purely monotheistic creed. It is a demonstrable fact that the primitive religions now open to observation attribute specific events and results to distinct supernatural beings; and there can be little doubt that this is the initial step in every creed. It is a bold and somewhat perilous revolution to attempt to overturn this doctrine and to set up monotheism in its place, and, when successfully accomplished, is rarely permanent. The more educated portions of the community maintain allegiance to the new teaching, perhaps; but among the lower classes it soon becomes degraded to, or amalgamated with, some form of polytheism more or less pronounced, and either secret or declared. Even the Jews, the nation the most conspicuous for its supposed uncompromising adherence to a monotheistic creed, cannot claim absolute freedom from taint in this respect; for in the country places, far from the centre of worship, the peoplewere constantly following after

strange gods; and even some of their most notable worthies were liable to the same accusation.

16. It is not necessary, however, that the individuality and specialization of function of the supreme beings recognized by any religious system should be so conspicuous as they are in this case, or in the Greek or Roman Pantheon, to mark it as in its essence polytheistic or of polytheistic tendency. It is quite enough that the immortals are deemed to be capable of hearing and answering the prayers of their adorers, and of interfering actively in passing events, either for good or for evil. This, at the root of it, constitutes the crucial difference between polytheism and monotheism; and in this sense the Roman Catholic form of Christianity, representing the oldest undisturbed evolution of a strictly monotheistic doctrine, is undeniably polytheistic. Apart from the Virgin Mary, there is a whole hierarchy of inferior deities, saints, and angels, subordinate to the One Supreme Being. This may possibly be denied by the authorized expounders of the doctrine of the Church of Rome; but it is nevertheless certain that it is the view taken by the uneducated classes, with whom the saints are much more present and definite deities than even the Almighty Himself. It is worth noting, that during the dancing mania of 1418, not God, or Christ, or the Virgin Mary, but St. Vitus, was prayed to by the populace to stop the epidemic that was afterwards known by his name.[1] There was a temple to St. Michael on Mount St. Angelo, and Augustine thought it necessary to declare that angel-worshippers were heretics.

[2] Even Protestantism, though a much younger growth than Catholicism, shows a slight tendency towards polytheism. The saints are, of course, quite out of the question, and angels are as far as possible relegated from the citadel of asserted belief into the vaguer regions of poetical sentimentality; but—although again unadmitted by the orthodox of the sect—the popular conception of Christ is, and, until the masses are more educated in theological niceties than they are at present, necessarily must be, as of a Supreme Being totally distinct from God the Father. This applies in a less degree to the third Person in the Trinity; less, because His individuality is less clear. George Eliot has, with her usual penetration, noted this fact in "Silas Marner," where, in Mrs. Winthrop's

simple theological system, the Trinity is always referred to as "Them."

[Footnote 1: Hecker, Epidemics of the Middle Ages, p. 85.]

[Footnote 2: Bullinger, p. 348. Parker Society.]

17. The posthumous history of Francis of Assisi affords a striking illustration of

this strange tendency towards polytheism. This extraordinary man received no little reverence and adulation during his lifetime; but it was not until after his death that the process of deification commenced. It was then discovered that the stigmata were not the only points of resemblance between the departed saint and the Divine Master he professed to follow; that his birth had been foretold by the prophets; that, like Christ, he underwent transfiguration; and that he had worked miracles during his life. The climax of the apotheosis was reached in 1486, when a monk, preaching at Paris, seriously maintained that St. Francis was in very truth a second Christ, the second Son of God; and that after his death he descended into purgatory, and liberated all the spirits confined there who had the good fortune to be arrayed in the Franciscan garb.[1]

[Footnote 1: Maury, Histoire de la Magie, p. 354.]

18. (ii.) The second principle is that of the Manichaeists: the division of spirits into hostile camps, good and evil. This is a much more common belief than the orthodox are willing to allow. There is hardly any religious system that does not recognize a first source of evil, as well as a first source of good. But the spirit of evil occupies a position of varying importance: in some systems he maintains himself as co-equal of the spirit of good; in others he sinks to a lower stage, remaining very powerful to do harm, but nevertheless under the control, in matters of the highest importance, of the more beneficent Being. In each of these cases, the first principle is found operating, ever augmenting the ranks; monodiabolism being as impossible as monotheism; and hence the importance of fully establishing that proposition.

19. (iii.) The last and most important of these principles is the tendency of all theological systems to absorb into themselves the deities extraneous to themselves, not as gods, but as inferior, or even evil, spirits. The actual existence of the foreign deity is not for a moment disputed, the presumption in favour of innumerable spiritual agencies being far too strong to allow the possibility of such a doubt; but just as the alien is looked upon as an inferior being, created chiefly for the use and benefit of the chosen people—and what nation is not, if its opinion of itself may be relied upon, a chosen people?—so the god the alien worships is a spirit of inferior power and capacity, and can be recognized solely as occupying a position subordinate to that of the gods of the land.

This principle has such an important influence in the elaboration of the belief in demons, that it is worth while to illustrate the generality of its application.

20. In the Greek system of theology we find in the first place a number of deities of varying importance and power, whose special functions are defined with some distinctness; and then, below these, an innumerable band of spirits, the souls of the departed—probably the relics of an earlier pure ancestor-worship—who still interest themselves in the inhabitants of this world. These [Greek: daimones]were certainly accredited with supernatural power, and were not of necessity either good or evil in their influence or action. It was to this second class that foreign deities were assimilated. They found it impossible, however, to retain even this humble position. The ceremonies of their worship, and the language in which those ceremonies were performed, were strange to the inhabitants of the land in which the acclimatization was attempted; and the incomprehensible is first suspected, then loathed. It is not surprising, then, that the new-comers soon fell into the ranks of purely evil spirits, and that those who persisted in exercising their rites were stigmatized as devil-worshippers, or magicians.

But in process of time this polytheistic system became pre-eminently unsatisfactory to the thoughtful men whom Greece produced in such numbers.

The tendency towards monotheism which is usually associated with the name of Plato is hinted at in the writings of other philosophers who were his predecessors. The effect of this revolution was to recognize one Supreme Being, the First Cause, and to subordinate to him all the other deities of the ancient and popular theology—to co-ordinate them, in fact, with the older class of daemons; the first step in the descent to the lowest category of all.

21. The history of the neo-Platonic belief is one of elaboration upon these ideas.

The conception of the Supreme Being was complicated in a manner closely resembling the idea of the Christian Trinity, and all the subordinate daemons were classified into good and evil geniuses. Thus, a theoretically monotheistic system was established, with a tremendous hierarchy of inferior spirits, who frequently bore the names of the ancient gods and goddesses of Egypt, Greece, and Rome, strikingly resembling that of Roman Catholicism. The subordinate daemons were not at first recognized as entitled to any religious rites; but in the course of time, by the inevitable operation of the first principle just enunciated, a form of theurgy sprang up with the object of attracting the kindly help and patronage of the good spirits, and was tolerated; and attempts were made to hold intercourse with the evil spirits, which were, as far as possible suppressed and discountenanced.

22. The history of the operation of this principle upon the Jewish religion is verysimilar, and extremely interesting. Although they do not seem to have ever had any system of ancestor-worship, as the Greeks had, yet the Jews appear originally to have recognized the deities of their neighbours as existing spirits, but inferior in power to the God of Israel. "All the gods of the nations are idols" are words that entirely fail to convey the idea of the Psalmist; for the word translated "idols" is *Elohim*, the very term usually employed to designate Jehovah; and the true sense of the passage therefore is: "All the gods of the nations are gods, but Jehovah made the heavens."[1] In another place we read that "The Lord is a great God, and a great King above all gods."[2] As, however, the

Jews gradually became acquainted with the barbarous rites with which their neighbours did honour to their gods, the foreigners seem to have fallen more and more in estimation, until they came to be classed as evil spirits. To this process such names as Beelzebub, Moloch, Ashtaroth, and Belial bear witness; Beelzebub, "the prince of the devils" of later time, being one of the gods of the hostile Philistines.

[Footnote 1: Psalm xcvi. 5 (xcv. Sept.).]

[Footnote 2: Psalm xcv. 3 (xciv. Sept.). Maury, p. 98.]

23. The introduction of Christianity made no difference in this respect. Paul says to the believers at Corinth, "that the things which the Gentiles sacrifice, they sacrifice to devils ([Greek: daimonia]), and not to God; and I would not that ye should have fellowship with devils;"[1] and the Septuagint renders the word *Elohim* in the ninety-fifth Psalm by this [Greek: daimonia], which as the Christians had already a distinct term for good spirits, came to be applied to evil ones only.

[Footnote 1: I Cor. x. 20.]

Under the influence therefore, of the new religion, the gods of Greece and Rome, who in the days of their supremacy had degraded so many foreign deities to the position of daemons, were in their turn deposed from their high estate, and became the nucleus around which the Christian belief in demonology formed itself. The gods who under the old theologies reigned paramount in the lower regions became pre-eminently diabolic in character in the new system, and it was Hecate who to the last retained her position of active patroness and encourager of witchcraft; a practice which became almost indissolubly connected with her name. Numerous instances of the completeness with whichthis process of diabolization was effected, and the firmness with which it retained its hold upon the popular belief, even to late times, might be given; but the following must suffice. In one of the miracle plays, "The Conversion of Saul," a council of devils is held, at which Mercury appears as the messenger of Belial.[1]

[Footnote 1: Digby Mysteries, New Shakspere Society, 1880, p. 44.]

24. But this absolute rejection of every pagan belief and ceremony was characteristic of the Christian Church in its infancy only. So long as the band of believers was a small and persecuted one, no temptation to violate the rule could exist. But as the Church grew, and acquired influence and position, it discovered that good policy demanded that the sternness and inflexibility of its youthful theories should undergo some modification. It found that it was not the most successful method of enticing stragglers into its fold to stigmatize the gods they ignorantly worshipped as devils, and to persecute them as magicians. The more impetuous and enthusiastic supporters did persecute, and persecute most relentlessly, the adherents of the dying faith; but persecution, whether of good or evil, always fails as a means of suppressing a hated doctrine, unless it can be carried to the extent of extermination of its supporters; and the more far-seeing leaders of the Catholic Church soon recognized that a slight surrender of principle was a far surer road to success than stubborn, uncompromising opposition.

25. It was in this spirit that the Catholics dealt with the oracles of heathendom.

Mr. Lecky is hardly correct when he says that nothing analogous to the ancient oracles was incorporated with Christianity.[1] There is the notable case of the god Sosthenion, whom Constantine identified with the archangel Michael, and whose oracular functions were continued in a precisely similar manner by the latter.[2] Oracles that were not thus absorbed and supported were recognized as existent, but under diabolic control, and to be tolerated, if not patronized, by the representatives of the dominant religion. The oracle at Delphi gave forth prophetic utterances for centuries after the commencement of the Christian era; and was the less dangerous, as its operations could be stopped at any moment by holding a saintly relic to the god or devil Apollo's nose. There is a fable that St.

Gregory, in the course of his travels, passed near the oracle, and his extraordinary sanctity was such as to prevent all subsequent utterances. This so disturbed the presiding genius of the place, that he appealed to the saint to undo the baneful effects his presence had produced; and Gregory benevolently wrote aletter to the devil, which was in fact a license to continue the business of prophesying unmolested.[3] This nonsensical fiction shows clearly enough that the oracles were not generally looked upon as extinguished by Christianity. As the result of a similar policy we find the names and functions of the pagan gods and the earlier Christian saints confused in the most extraordinary manner; the saints assuming the duties of the moribund deities where those duties were of a harmless or necessary character.[4]

[Footnote 1: Rise and Influence of Rationalism, i. p. 31.]

[Footnote 2: Maury, p. 244, et seq.]

[Footnote 3: Scot, book vii. ch. i.]

[Footnote 4: Middleton's Letter from Rome.]

26. The Church carried out exactly the same principles in her missionary efforts amongst the heathen hordes of Northern Europe. "Do you renounce the devils, and all their words and works; Thonar, Wodin, and Saxenote?" was part of the form of recantation administered to the Scandinavian converts;[1] and at the present day "Odin take you" is the Norse equivalent of "the devil take you." On the other hand, an attempt was made to identify Balda "the beautiful" with Christ

—a confusion of character that may go far towards accounting for a custom joyously observed by our forefathers at Christmastide but which the false modesty of modern society has nearly succeeded in banishing from amongst us, for Balda was slain by Loké with a branch of mistletoe, and Christ was betrayed by Judas with a kiss.

[Footnote 1: Milman, History of Latin Christianity, iii. 267; ix.

27. Upon the conversion of the inhabitants of Great Britain to Christianity, the native deities underwent the same inevitable fate, and sank into the rank of evil spirits. Perhaps the juster opinion is that they became the progenitors of our fairy mythology rather than the subsequent devil-lore, although the similarity between these two classes of spirits is sufficient to warrant us in classing them as species of the same genus; their characters and functions being perfectly interchangeable, and even at times merging and becoming indistinguishable. A certain lurking affection in the new converts for the religion they had deserted, perhaps under compulsion, may have led them to look upon their ancient objects of veneration as less detestable in nature, and dangerous in act, than the devilsimported as an integral portion of their adopted faith; and so originated this class of spirits less evil than the other. Sir Walter Scott may be correct in his assertion that many of these fairy-myths owe their origin to the existence of a diminutive autochthonic race that was conquered by the invading Celts, and the remnants of which lurked about the mountains and forests, and excited in their victors a superstitious reverence on account of their great skill in metallurgy; but this will not explain the retention of many of the old god-names; as that of the Dusii, the Celtic nocturnal spirits, in our word "deuce," and that of the Nikr or water-spirits in "nixie" and old "Nick."[1] These words undoubtedly indicate the accomplishment of the "facilis descensus Averno" by the native deities. Elves, brownies, gnomes, and trolds were all at one time Scotch or Irish gods. The trolds obtained a character similar to that of the more modern succubus, and have left their impression upon Elizabethan English in the word "trull."

[Footnote 1: Maury, p. 189.]

28. The preceding very superficial outline of the growth of the belief in evil spirits is enough for the purpose of this essay, as it shows that the basis of English devil-lore was the annihilated mythologies of the ancient heathen religions—Italic and Teutonic, as well as those brought into direct conflict with the Jewish system; and also that the more

important of the Teutonic deities are not to be traced in the subsequent hierarchy of fiends, on account probably of their temporary or permanent absorption into the proselytizing system, or the refusal of the new converts to believe them to be so black as their teachers painted them. The gradual growth of the superstructure it would be well-nigh impossible and quite unprofitable to trace. It is due chiefly to the credulous ignorance and distorted imagination, monkish and otherwise, of several centuries. Carlyle's graphic picture of Abbot Sampson's vision of the devil in

"Past and Present" will perhaps do more to explain how the belief grew and flourished than pages of explanatory statements. It is worthy of remark, however, that to the last, communication with evil spirits was kept up by means of formulae and rites that are undeniably the remnants of a form of religious worship. Incomprehensible in their jargon as these formulae mostly are, and strongly tinctured as they have become with burlesqued Christian symbolism and expression—for those who used them could only supply the fast-dying memory of the elder forms from the existing system—they still, in all their grotesqueness, remain the battered relics of a dead faith.

29. Such being the natural history of the conflict of religions, it will not be amatter of surprise that the leaders of our English Reformation should, in their turn, have attributed the miracles of the Roman Catholic saints to the same infernal source as the early Christians supposed to have been the origin of the prodigies and oracles of paganism. The impulse given by the secession from the Church of Rome to the study of the Bible by all classes added impetus to this tendency. In Holy Writ the Reformers found full authority for believing in the existence of evil spirits, possession by devils, witchcraft, and divine and diabolic interference by way of miracle generally; and they consequently acknowledged the possibility of the repetition of such phenomena in the times in which they lived—a position more tenable, perhaps, than that of modern orthodoxy, that accepts without murmur all the supernatural events recorded in the Bible, and utterly rejects all subsequent relations of a similar nature, however well authenticated. The Reformers believed unswervingly in the

truth of the Biblical accounts of miracles, and that what God had once permitted to take place might and would be repeated in case of serious necessity. But they found it utterly impossible to accept the puerile and meaningless miracles perpetrated under the auspices of the Roman Catholic Church as evidence of divine interference; and they had not travelled far enough upon the road towards rationalism to be able to reject them, one and all, as in their very nature impossible. The consequence of this was one of those compromises which we so often meet with in the history of the changes of opinion effected by the Reformation. Only those particular miracles that were indisputably demonstrated to be impostures —and there were plenty of them, such as the Rood of Boxley[1]—were treated as such by them.

The unexposed remainder were treated as genuine supernatural phenomena, but caused by diabolical, not divine, agency. The reforming divine Calfhill, supporting this view of the Catholic miracles in his answer to Martiall's "Treatise of the Cross," points out that the majority of supernatural events that have taken place in this world have been, most undoubtedly, the work of the devil; and puts his opponents into a rather embarrassing dilemma by citing the miracles of paganism, which both Catholic and Protestant concurred in attributing to the evil one. He then clinches his argument by asserting that "it is the devil's cunning that persuades those that will walk in a popish blindness" that they are worshipping God when they are in reality serving him. "Therefore," he continues, consciously following an argument of St. Cyprianus against the pagan miracles, "these wicked spirits do lurk in shrines, in roods, in crosses, in images: and first of all pervert the priests, which are easiest to be caught with bait of a little gain. Then work they miracles. They appear to men in divers shapes; disquiet them when they are awake; trouble them in their sleeps; distort their members; take away their health; afflict them with diseases; only to bring them to some idolatry.

Thus, when they have obtained their purpose that a lewd affiance is reposed where it should not, they enter (as it were) into a new league, and trouble them no more. What do the simple people then? Verily suppose that the image, the cross, the thing that they have kneeled and offered unto (the very devil indeed) hath restored them health, whereas he did nothing but leave off to molest them.

This is the help and cure that the devils give when they leave off their wrong and injury."[2]

[Footnote 1: Froude, History of England, cabinet edition, iii. 102.]

[Footnote 2: Calfhill, pp. 317-8. Parker Society.]

30. Here we have a distinct charge of devil-worship—the old doctrine cropping up again after centuries of repose: "all the gods of our opponents are devils." Nor were the Catholics a whit behind the Protestants in this matter. The priests zealously taught that the Protestants were devil-worshippers and magicians;[1]and the common people so implicitly believed in the truth of the statement, that we find one poor prisoner, taken by the Dutch at the siege of Alkmaar in 1578, making a desperate attempt to save his life by promising to worship his captors'

devil precisely as they did[2]—a suggestion that failed to pacify those to whom it was addressed.

[Footnote 1: Hutchinson's Essay, p. 218. Harsnet, Declaration, p. 30.]

[Footnote 2: Motley, Dutch Republic, ii. 400.]

31. Having thus stated, so far as necessary, the chief laws that are constantly working the extension of the domain of the supernatural as far as demonology is concerned, without a remembrance of which the subject itself would remain somewhat difficult to comprehend fully, I shall now attempt to indicate one or two conditions of thought and circumstance that may have tended to increase and vivify the belief during the period in which the Elizabethan literature flourished.

32. It was an era of change. The nation was emerging from the

dim twilight of mediaevalism into the full day of political and religious freedom. But the morning mists, which the rising sun had not yet dispelled, rendered the more distant and complex objects distorted and portentous. The very fact that doubt, or rather, perhaps, independence of thought, was at last, within certain limits, treated as non-criminal in theology, gave an impetus to investigation andspeculation in all branches of politics and science; and with this change came, in the main, improvement. But the great defect of the time was that this newly liberated spirit of free inquiry was not kept in check by any sufficient previous discipline in logical methods of reasoning. Hence the possibility of the wild theories that then existed, followed out into action or not, according as circumstances favoured or discouraged: Arthur Hacket, with casting out of devils, and other madnesses, vehemently declaring himself the Messiah and King of Europe in the year of grace 1591, and getting himself believed by some, so long as he remained unhanged; or, more pathetic still, many weary lives wasted day by day in fruitless silent search after the impossible philosopher's stone, or elixir of life. As in law, so in science, there were no sufficient rules of evidence clearly and unmistakably laid down for the guidance of the investigator; and consequently it was only necessary to broach a novel theory in order to have it accepted, without any previous serious testing. Men do not seem to have been able to distinguish between an hypothesis and a proved conclusion; or, rather, the rule of presumptions was reversed, and men accepted the hypothesis as conclusive until it was disproved. It was a perfectly rational and sufficient explanation in those days to refer some extraordinary event to some given supernatural cause, even though there might be no ostensible link between the two: now, such a suggestion would be treated by the vast majority with derision or contempt. On the other hand, the most trivial occurrences, such as sneezing, the appearance of birds of ill omen, the crowing of a cock, and events of like unimportance happening at a particular moment, might, by some unseen concatenation of causes and effects, exercise an incomprehensible influence upon men, and consequently had important bearings upon their conduct. It is solemnly recorded in the Commons' Journals that during the discussion of the statute against witchcraft passed in the reign of James I., a young jackdaw flew into the House; which accident was generally regarded as *malum omen* to the Bill.[1] Extraordinary bravery on the part of an adversary was sometimes accounted for by asserting that he was the devil in the form of a man; as the Volscian soldier does with regard to Coriolanus. This is no mere dramatist's fancy, but a fixed belief of the times. Sir William Russell fought so desperately at Zutphen, that he got mistaken for the Evil One;[2] and Drake also gave the Spaniards good reason for believing that he was a devil, and no man.[3]

[Footnote 1: See also D'Ewes, p. 688.]

[Footnote 2: Froude, xii. 87.]

[Footnote 3: Ibid. 663.]

33. This intense credulousness, childish almost in itself, but yet at the same time combined with the strong man's intellect, permeated all classes of society.

Perhaps a couple of instances, drawn from strangely diverse sources, will bring this more vividly before the mind than any amount of attempted theorizing. The first is one of the tricks of the jugglers of the period.

"*To make one danse naked.*

"Make a poore boie confederate with you, so as after charms, etc., spoken by you, he unclothe himself and stand naked, seeming (whilest he undresseth himselfe) to shake, stamp, and crie, still hastening to be unclothed, till he be starke naked; or if you can procure none to go so far, let him onlie beginne to stampe and shake, etc., and unclothe him, and then you may (for reverence of the companie) seeme to release him."[1]

[Footnote 1: Scott, p. 339.]

The second illustration must have demanded, if possible, more credulity on the part of the audience than this harmless entertainment. Cranmer tells us that in the time of Queen Mary a monk preached a sermon at St. Paul's, the object of which was to prove the truth of the doctrine of transubstantiation; and, after the manner of his kind, told the following little anecdote in support of it:—"A maid of Northgate parish in Canterbury, in pretence to wipe her mouth, kept the host in her handkerchief; and, when she came home, she put the same into a pot, close covered, and she spitted in another pot, and after a few days, she looking in the one pot, found a little young pretty babe, about a shaftmond long; and the other pot was full of gore blood."[1]

[Footnote 1: Cranmer, A Confutation of Unwritten Verities, p. 66. Parker Society.]

34. That the audiences before which these absurdities were seriously brought, for amusement or instruction, could be excited in either case to any other feeling than good-natured contempt for a would-be impostor, seems to us now-a-days to be impossible. It was not so in the times when these things transpired: the actors of them were not knaves, nor were their audiences fools, to any unusual extent.

If any one is inclined to form a low opinion of the Elizabethans intellectually, on account of the divergence of their capacities of belief in this respect from his

own, he does them a great injustice. Let him take at once Charles Lamb's warning, and try to understand, rather than to judge them. We, who have had the benefit of three hundred more years of experience and liberty of thought than they, should have to hide our faces for very shame had we not arrived at juster and truer conclusions upon those difficult topics that so bewildered our ancestors. But can we, with all our boasted advantages of wealth, power, and knowledge, truly say that all our aims are as high, all our desires as pure, our words as true, and our deeds as noble, as those whose opinions we feel this tendency to contemn? If not, or if indeed they have anything whatsoever to teach us in these respects, let us remember that we shall never learn the lesson wholly, perhaps not learn it at all, unless, casting aside this first impulse to despise, we try to enter fully into and understand these strange dead beliefs of the past.

* * * * *

35. It is in this spirit that I now enter upon the second division of the subject in hand, in which I shall try to indicate the chief features of the belief in demonology as it existed during the Elizabethan period. These will be taken up in three main heads: the classification, physical appearance, and powers of the evil spirits.

36. (i.) It is difficult to discover any classification of devils as well authenticated and as universally received as that of the angels introduced by Dionysius the Areopagite, which was subsequently imported into the creed of the Western Church, and popularized in Elizabethan times by Dekker's "Hierarchie." The subject was one which, from its nature, could not be settled *ex cathedrâ*, and consequently the subject had to grow up as best it might, each writer adopting the arrangement that appeared to him most suitable. There was one rough but popular classification into greater and lesser devils. The former branch was subdivided into classes of various grades of power, the members of which passed under the titles of kings, dukes, marquises, lords, captains, and other dignities.

Each of these was supposed to have a certain number of legions of the latter class under his command. These were the evil spirits who appeared most frequently on the earth as the emissaries of the greater fiends, to carry out their evil designs. The more important class kept for the most part in a mystical seclusion, and only appeared upon earth in cases of the greatest emergency, or when compelled to do so by conjuration. To the class of lesser devils belonged the bad angel which, together with a good one, was supposed to be assigned to every person at birth, to follow him through life—the one to tempt, the other toguard from temptation;[1] so that a struggle similar to that recorded between Michael and Satan for the body of Moses was raging for the soul of every existing human being. This was not a mere theory, but a vital active belief, as the beautiful well-known lines at the commencement of the eighth canto of the second book of "The Faerie Queene," and the use made of these opposing spirits in Marlowe's "Dr. Faustus," and in "The Virgin Martyr," by Massinger and Dekker, conclusively show.

37. Another classification, which seems to retain a reminiscence of the origin of devils from pagan deities, is effected by reference to the localities supposed to be inhabited by the different classes of evil spirits. According to this arrangement we get six classes:—

(1.) Devils of the fire, who wander in the region near the moon.

(2.) Devils of the air, who hover round the earth.

(3.) Devils of the earth; to whom the fairies are allied.

(4.) Devils of the water.

(5.) Submundane devils.[1]

(6.) Lucifugi.

These devils' power and desire to injure mankind appear to have increased with the proximity of their location to the earth's centre; but this classification had nothing like the hold upon the popular mind that the former grouping had, and may consequently be dismissed with this mention.

[Footnote 1: Cf. I Hen. VI. V. iii. 10; 2 Hen. VI. I. ii. 77; Coriolanus, IV. v. 97.]

38. The greater devils, or the most important of them, had distinguishing names—strange, uncouth names; some of them telling of a heathenish origin; others inexplicable and almost unpronounceable—as Ashtaroth, Bael, Belial, Zephar, Cerberus, Phoenix, Balam (why he?), and Haagenti, Leraie, Marchosias, Gusoin, Glasya Labolas. Scot enumerates seventy-nine, the above amongst them, and he

does not by any means exhaust the number. As each arch-devil had twenty, thirty, or forty legions of inferior spirits under his command, and a legion was composed of six hundred and sixty-six devils, it is not surprising that the latter did not obtain distinguishing names until they made their appearance upon earth, when they frequently obtained one from the form they loved to assume; for example, the familiars of the witches in "Macbeth"—Paddock (toad), Graymalkin (cat), and Harpier (harpy, possibly). Is it surprising that, with resources of this nature at his command, such an adept in the art of necromancy as Owen Glendower should hold Harry Percy, much to his disgust, at the least nine hours

"In reckoning up the several devils' names

That were his lackeys"?

Of the twenty devils mentioned by Shakspere, four only belong to the class of greater devils. Hecate, the principal patroness of witchcraft, is referred to frequently, and appears once upon the scene.[1] The two others are Amaimon and Barbazon, both of whom are mentioned twice. Amaimon was a very important personage, being no other than one of the four kings. Ziminar was King of the North, and is referred to in "Henry VI. Part I.;"[2] Gorson of the South; Goap of the West; and Amaimon of the East. He is mentioned in "Henry IV. Part I.,"[3] and "Merry Wives."[4] Barbazon also occurs in the same passage in the latter play, and again in "Henry V."[5]—a fact that does to a slight extent help to bear out the otherwise ascertained chronological sequence of these plays.

The remainder of the devils belong to the second class. Nine of these occur in

"King Lear," and will be referred to again when the subject of possession is touched upon.[6]

[Footnote 1: It is perhaps worthy of remark that in every case except the allusion in the probably spurious Henry VI., "I speak not to that railing Hecate," (I Hen.

VI. III. ii. 64), the name is "Hecat," a di-syllable.]

[Footnote 2: V. iii. 6.]

[Footnote 3: II. iv. 370.]

[Footnote 4: II. ii. 311.]

[Footnote 5: II. i. 57. Scot, p. 393.]

[Footnote 6: § 65.]

39. (ii.) It would appear that each of the greater devils, on the rare occasion upon which he made his appearance upon earth, assumed a form peculiar to himself; the lesser devils, on the other hand, had an ordinary type, common to the whole species, with a capacity for almost infinite variation and transmutation which they used, as will be seen, to the extreme perplexity and annoyance of mortals.

As an illustration of the form in which a greater devil might appear, this is what Scot says of the questionable Balam, above mentioned: "Balam cometh with three heads, the first of a bull, the second of a man, and the third of a ram. He hath a serpent's taile, and flaming eies; riding upon a furious beare, and carrieng a hawke on his fist."[1] But it was the lesser devils, not the greater, that came into close contact with humanity, who therefore demand careful consideration.

[Footnote 1: p. 361.]

40. All the lesser devils seem to have possessed a normal form, which was as hideous and distorted as fancy could render it. To the conception of an angel imagination has given the only beautiful appendage the human body does not possess—wings; to that of a devil it has added all those organs of the brute creation that are most hideous or most harmful. Advancing civilization has almost exterminated the belief in a being with horns, cloven hoofs, goggle eyes, and scaly tail, that was

held up to many yet living as the avenger of childish disobedience in their earlier days, together perhaps with some strength of conviction of the moral hideousness of the evil he was intended, in a rough way, to typify; but this hazily retained impression of the Author of Evil was the universal and entirely credited conception of the ordinary appearance of those bad spirits who were so real to our ancestors of Elizabethan days. "Some are so carnallie minded," says Scot, "that a spirit is no sooner spoken of, but they thinke of a blacke man with cloven feet, a paire of hornes, a taile, and eies as big as a bason."[1] Scot, however, was one of a very small minority in his opinion as to the carnal-mindedness of such a belief. He in his day, like those in every age and country who dare to hold convictions opposed to the creed of the majority, was a dangerous sceptic; his book was publicly burnt by the common hangman;[2] and not long afterwards a royal author wrote a treatise "against the damnable doctrines of two principally in our age; whereof the one, called Scot, an Englishman, is not ashamed in public print to deny that there can be such a thing as witchcraft, and so mainteines the old error of the Sadducees in denying of spirits."[3] The abandoned impudence of the man!—and the logic of his royal

opponent!

[Footnote 1: p. 507. See also Hutchinson, Essay on Witchcraft, p. 13; and Harsnet, p. 71.]

[Footnote 2: Bayle, ix. 152.]

[Footnote 3: James I., Daemonologie. Edinburgh, 1597.]

41. Spenser has clothed with horror this conception of the appearance of a fiend, just as he has enshrined in beauty the belief in the guardian angel. It is worthy of remark that he describes the devil as dwelling beneath the altar of an idol in a heathen temple. Prince Arthur strikes the image thrice with his sword—

"And the third time, out of an hidden shade, There forth issewed from under th' altar's smoake A dreadfull feend with fowle deformèd looke,

That stretched itselfe as it had long lyen still; And her long taile and fethers strongly shooke,

That all the temple did with terrour fill;

Yet him nought terrifide that fearèd nothing ill.

"An huge great beast it was, when it in length Was stretchèd forth, that nigh filled all the place, And seemed to be of infinite great strength;

Horrible, hideous, and of hellish race,

Borne of the brooding of Echidna base,

Or other like infernall Furies kinde,

For of a maide she had the outward face

To hide the horrour which did lurke behinde

The better to beguile whom she so fond did finde.

"Thereto the body of a dog she had,

Full of fell ravin and fierce greedinesse;

A lion's clawes, with power and rigour clad

To rende and teare whatso she can oppresse;

A dragon's taile, whose sting without redresse

Full deadly wounds whereso it is empight,

And eagle's wings for scope and speedinesse

That nothing may escape her reaching might,

Whereto she ever list to make her hardy flight."

42. The dramatists of the period make frequent references to this belief, but nearly always by way of ridicule. It is hardly to be expected that they would share in the grosser opinions held by the common people in those times—common, whether king or clown. In "The Virgin Martyr," Harpax is made to say

—

"I'll tell you what now of the devil;

He's no such horrid creature, cloven-footed,

Black, saucer-eyed, his nostrils breathing fire,

As these lying Christians make him."[1]

But his opinion was, perhaps, a prejudiced one. In Ben Jonson's "The Devil is an Ass," when Fitzdottrell, doubting Pug's statement as to his infernal character, says, "I looked on your feet afore; you cannot cozen me; your shoes are not cloven, sir, you are whole hoofed;" Pug, with great presence of mind, replies,

"Sir, that's a popular error deceives many." So too Othello, when he is questioning whether Iago is a devil or not, says—

"I look down to his feet, but that's a fable."[2]

And when Edgar is trying to persuade the blind Gloucester that he has in reality cast himself over the cliff, he describes the being from whom he is supposed to have just parted, thus:—

"As I stood here below, methought his eyes

Were two full moons: he had a thousand noses;

Horns whelked and wavèd like the enridgèd sea:

It was some fiend."[3]

It can hardly be but that the "thousand noses" are intended as a satirical hit at the enormity of the popular belief.

[Footnote 1: Act I. sc. 2.]

[Footnote 2: Act V. sc. ii. l. 285.]

[Footnote 3: Lear, IV. vi. 69.]

43. In addition to this normal type, common to all these devils, each one seems

to have had, like the greater devils, a favourite form in which he made his appearance when conjured; generally that of some animal, real or imagined. It was telling of

"the moldwarp and the ant,

Of the dreamer Merlin, and his prophecies;

And of a dragon and a finless fish,

A clipwinged griffin, and a moulten raven,

A couching lion, and a ramping cat,"[1]

that annoyed Harry Hotspur so terribly; and neither in this allusion, which was suggested by a passage in Holinshed,[2] nor in

"Macbeth," where he makes the three witches conjure up their familiars in the shapes of an armed head, a bloody child, and a child crowned, has Shakspere gone beyond the fantastic conceptions of the time.

[Footnote 1: I Hen. IV. III. i. 148.]

[Footnote 2: p. 521, c. 2.]

44. (iii.) But the third proposed section, which deals with the powers and functions exercised by the evil spirits, is by far the most interesting and important; and the first branch of the series is one that suggests itself as a natural sequence upon what has just been said as to the ordinary shapes in which devils appeared, namely, the capacity to assume at will any form they chose.

45. In the early and middle ages it was universally believed that a devil could, of his own inherent power, call into existence any manner of body that it pleased his fancy to inhabit, or that would most conduce to the success of any contemplated evil. In consequence of this belief the devils became the rivals, indeed the successful rivals, of Jupiter himself in the art of physical tergiversation. There was, indeed, a tradition that a devil could not create any animal form of less size than a barley-corn, and that it was in consequence of this incapacity that the magicians of Egypt—those indubitable devil-worshippers

—failed to produce lice, as Moses did, although they had been so successful in the matter of the serpents and the frogs; "a verie gross absurditie," as Scot judiciously remarks.[1] This, however, would not be a serious limitation upon the practical usefulness of the power.

[Footnote 1: p. 314.]

46. The great Reformation movement wrought a change in this respect. Men began to accept argument and reason, though savouring of special pleading of the schools, in preference to tradition, though never so venerable and well authenticated; and the leaders of the revolution could

not but recognize the absurdity of laying down as infallible dogma that God was the Creator of all things, and then insisting with equal vehemence, by way of postulate, that the devil was the originator of some. The thing was gross and palpable in its absurdity, and had to be done away with as quickly as might be. But how? On the other hand, it was clear as daylight that the devil *did* appear in various forms to tempt and annoy the people of God—was at that very time doing so in the most open and unabashed manner. How were reasonable men to account for this manifest conflict between rigorous logic and more rigorous fact? There was a prolonged and violent controversy upon the point—the Reformers not seeing their way to agree amongst themselves—and tedious as violent. Sermons were preached; books were written; and, when argument was exhausted, unpleasant epithets were bandied about, much as in the present day, in similar cases. The result was that two theories were evolved, both extremely interesting as illustrations of the hair-splitting, chop-logic tendency which, amidst all their straightforwardness, was so strongly characteristic of the Elizabethans. The first suggestion was, that although the devil could not, of his own inherent power, create a body, he might get hold of a dead carcase and temporarily restore animation, and so serve his turn. This belief was held, amongst others, by the erudite King James,[1] and is pleasantly satirized by sturdy old Ben Jonson in

"The Devil is an Ass," where Satan (the greater devil, who only appears in the first scene just to set the storm a-brewing) says to Pug (Puck, the lesser devil, who does all the mischief; or would have done it, had not man, in those latter times, got to be rather beyond the devils in evil than otherwise), not without a touch of regret at the waning of his power—

"You must get a body ready-made, Pug,

I can create you none;"

and consequently Pug is advised to assume the body of a handsome cutpurse that morning hung at Tyburn.

[Footnote 1: Daemonologie, p. 56.]

But the theory, though ingenious, was insufficient. The devil would occasionally appear in the likeness of a living person; and how could that be accounted for?

Again, an evil spirit, with all his ingenuity, would find it hard to discover the dead body of a griffin, or a harpy, or of such eccentricity as was affected by the before-mentioned Balam; and these and other similar forms were commonly favoured by the inhabitants of the nether world.

47. The second theory, therefore, became the more popular amongst the learned, because it left no one point unexplained. The divines held that although the power of the Creator had in no wise been delegated to the devil, yet he was, in the course of providence, permitted to exercise a certain supernatural influence over the minds of men, whereby he could persuade them that they really saw a form that had no material objective existence.[1] Here was a position incontrovertible, not on account of the arguments by which it could be supported, but because it was impossible to reason against it; and it slowly, but surely, took hold upon the popular mind. Indeed, the elimination of the diabolic factor leaves the modern sceptical belief that such apparitions are nothing more than the result of disease, physical or mental.

[Footnote 1: Dialogicall Discourses, by Deacon and Walker, 4th Dialogue.

Bullinger, p. 361. Parker Society.]

48. But the semi-sceptical state of thought was in Shakspere's time making its way only amongst the more educated portion of the nation. The masses still clung to the old and venerated, if not venerable, belief that devils could at any moment assume what form soever they might please—not troubling themselves further to inquire into the method of the operation. They could appear in the likeness of an ordinary human being, as Harpax[1] and Mephistopheles[2] do, creating thereby

the most embarrassing complications in questions of identity; and if this belief is borne in mind, the charge of being a devil, so freely made, in the times of which we write, and before alluded to, against persons who performed extraordinary feats of valour, or behaved in a manner discreditable and deserving of general reprobation, loses much of its barbarous grotesqueness.

There was no doubt as to Coriolanus,[3] as has been said; nor Shylock.[4] Even

"the outward sainted Angelo is yet a devil;"[5] and Prince Hal confesses that

"there is a devil haunts him in the likeness of an old fat man ... an old white-bearded Satan."[6]

[Footnote 1: In The Virgin Martyr.]

[Footnote 2: In Dr. Faustus.]

[Footnote 3: Coriolanus, I. x. 16.]

[Footnote 4: Merchant of Venice, III. i. 22.]

[Footnote 5: Measure for Measure, III. i. 90.]

[Footnote 6: I Hen. IV., II. iv. 491-509.]

49. The devils had an inconvenient habit of appearing in the guise of an ecclesiastic[1]—at least, so the churchmen were careful to insist, especially when busying themselves about acts of temptation that would least become the holy robe they had assumed. This was the ecclesiastical method of accounting for certain stories, not very creditable to the priesthood, that had too inconvenient a basis of evidence to be dismissed as fabricatious. But the honest lay public seem to have thought, with downright old Chaucer, that there was more in the matter than the priests

chose to admit. This feeling we, as usual, find reflected in the dramatic literature of our period. In "The Troublesome Raigne of King John," an old play upon the basis of which Shakspere constructed his own

"King John," we find this question dealt with in some detail. In the elder play, the Bastard does "the shaking of bags of hoarding abbots,"*coram populo*, and thereby discloses a phase of monastic life judiciously suppressed by Shakspere.

Philip sets at liberty much more than "imprisoned angels"— according to one account, and that a monk's, imprisoned beings of quite another sort. "Faire Alice, the nonne," having been discovered in the chest where the abbot's wealth was supposed to be concealed, proposes to purchase pardon for the offence by disclosing the secret hoard of a sister nun. Her offer being accepted, a friar is ordered to force the box in which the treasure is supposed to be secreted. On being questioned as to its contents, he answers—

"Frier Laurence, my lord, now holy water help us!

Some witch or some divell is sent to delude us:

Haud credo Laurentius that thou shouldst be pen'd thus In the presse of a nun; we are all undone,

And brought to discredence, if thou be Frier Laurence."[2]

Unfortunately it proves indubitably to be that good man; and he is ordered to execution, not, however, without some hope of redemption by money payment; for times are hard, and cash in hand not to be despised.

[Footnote 1: See the story about Bishop Sylvanus.—Lecky, Rationalism in

Europe, i. 79.]

[Footnote 2: Hazlitt, Shakspere Library, part ii. vol. i. p. 264.]

It is amusing to notice, too, that when assuming the clerical garb, the devil carefully considered the religious creed of the person to whom he intended to make himself known. The Catholic accounts of him show him generally assuming the form of a Protestant parson;[1] whilst to those of the reformed creed he invariably appeared in the habit of a Catholic priest. In the semblance of a friar the devil is reported (by a Protestant) to have preached, upon a time, "a verie Catholic sermon;"[2] so good, indeed, that a priest who was a listener could find no fault with the doctrine—a stronger basis of fact than one would have imagined for Shakspere's saying, "The devil can cite Scripture for his purpose."

[Footnote 1: Harsnet, p. 101.]

[Footnote 2: Scot, p. 481.]

50. It is not surprising that of human forms, that of a negro or Moor should be considered a favourite one with evil spirits.[1] Iago makes allusion to this when inciting Brabantio to search for his daughter. [2] The power of coming in the likeness of humanity generally is referred to somewhat cynically in "Timon of Athens,"[3] thus—

"*Varro's Servant.* What is a whoremaster, fool?

"*Fool.* A fool in good clothes, and something like thee. 'Tis a spirit: sometime 't appears like a lord; sometime like a lawyer; sometime like a philosopher with two stones more than 's artificial one: he is very often like a knight; and, generally, in all shapes that man goes up and down in, from fourscore to thirteen, this spirit walks in."

[Footnote 1: Scot, p. 89.]

[Footnote 2: Othello, I. i. 91.]

[Footnote 3: II. ii. 113.]

"All shapes that man goes up and down in" seem indeed to have been at the

devils' control. So entirely was this the case, that to Constance even the fair Blanche was none other than the devil tempting Louis "in likeness of a new uptrimmed bride;"[1] and perhaps not without a certain prophetic feeling of the fitness of things, as it may possibly seem to some of our more warlike politicians, evil spirits have been known to appear as Russians.[2]

[Footnote 1: King John, III. i. 209.]

[Footnote 2: Harsnet, p. 139.]

51. But all the "shapes that man goes up and down in" did not suffice. The forms of the whole of the animal kingdom seem to have been at the devils' disposal; and, not content with these, they seem to have sought further for unlikely shapes to assume.[1] Poor Caliban complains that Prospero's spirits

"Lead me, like a firebrand, in the dark,"[2]

just as Ariel[3] and Puck[4] (Will-o'-th'-wisp) mislead their victims; and that

"For every trifle are they set upon me:

Sometimes like apes, that mow and chatter at me,

And after bite me; then like hedgehogs, which

Lie tumbling in my barefoot way, and mount

Their pricks at my footfall. Sometime am I

All wound with adders, who, with cloven tongues,

Do hiss me into madness."

And doubtless the scene which follows this soliloquy, in which Caliban, Trinculo, and Stephano mistake one another in turn for evil spirits, fully flavoured with fun as it still remains, had far more point for the audiences at the Globe—to whom a stray devil or two was quite in the natural order of things under such circumstances—than it can possibly possess for us. In this play, Ariel, Prospero's familiar, besides appearing in his natural shape, and dividing into flames, and behaving in such a manner as to cause young Ferdinand to leap into the sea, crying, "Hell is empty, and all the devils are here!" assumes the forms of a water-nymph,[5] a harpy,[6] and also the goddess Ceres;[7] while the strange shapes, masquers, and even the hounds that hunt and worry the would-be king and viceroys of the island, are Ariel's "meaner fellows."

[Footnote 1: For instance, an eye without a head.—Ibid.]

[Footnote 2: The Tempest, II. ii. 10.]

[Footnote 3: Ibid. I. ii. 198.]

[Footnote 4: A Midsummer Night's Dream, II. i. 39; III. i. 111.]

[Footnote 5: I. ii. 301-318.]

[Footnote 6: III. iii. 53.]

[Footnote 7: IV. i. 166.]

52. Puck's favourite forms seem to have been more outlandish than Ariel's, as might have been expected of that malicious little spirit. He beguiles "the fat and bean-fed horse" by

"Neighing in likeness of a filly foal:

And sometimes lurk I in a gossip's bowl,

In very likeness of a roasted crab;

And when she drinks, against her lips I bob,

And on her withered dewlap pour the ale.

The wisest aunt, telling the saddest tale,

Sometime for three-foot stool[1] mistaketh me;

Then slip I from her, and down topples she."

And again:

"Sometime a horse I'll be, sometime a hound, A hog, a headless bear, sometime a fire;

And neigh, and bark, and grunt, and roar, and burn, Like horse, hound, hog, bear, fire, at every turn."[2]

With regard to this last passage, it is worthy of note that in the year 1584, strange news came out of Somersetshire, entitled "A Dreadful Discourse of the Dispossessing of one Margaret Cowper, at Ditchet, from a Devil in the Likeness of a Headless Bear."[3]

[Footnote 1: A Scotch witch, when leaving her bed to go to a sabbath, used to put a three-foot stool in the vacant place; which, after charms duly mumbled, assumed the appearance of a woman until her return.—Pitcairn, iii. 617.]

[Footnote 2: III. i. 111.]

[Footnote 3: Hutchinson, p. 40.]

53. In Heywood and Brome's "Witch of Edmonton," the devil appears in the likeness of a black dog, and takes his part in the dialogue,

as if his presence were a matter of quite ordinary occurrence, not in any way calling for special remark.

However gross and absurd this may appear, it must be remembered that this play is, in its minutest details, merely a dramatization of the events duly proved in a court of law, to the satisfaction of twelve Englishmen, in the year 1612.[1] The shape of a fly, too, was a favourite one with the evil spirits; so much so that the term "fly" became a common synonym for a familiar.[2] The word "Beelzebub"

was supposed to mean "the king of flies." At the execution of Urban Grandier, the famous magician of London, in 1634, a large fly was seen buzzing about the stake, and a priest promptly seizing the opportunity of improving the occasion for the benefit of the onlookers, declared that Beelzebub had come in his own proper person to carry off Grandier's soul to hell. In 1664 occurred the celebrated witch-trials which took place before Sir Matthew Hale. The accused were charged with bewitching two children; and part of the evidence against them was that flies and bees were seen to carry into the victims' mouths the nails and pins which they afterwards vomited.[3] There is an allusion to this belief in the fly-killing scene in "Titus Andronicus."[4]

[Footnote 1: Potts, Discoveries. Edit. Cheetham Society.]

[Footnote 2: Cf. B. Jonson's Alchemist.]

[Footnote 3: A Collection of Rare and Curious Tracts relating to Witchcraft, 1838.]

[Footnote 4: III. ii. 51, et seq.]

54. But it was not invariably a repulsive or ridiculous form that was assumed by these enemies of mankind. Their ingenuity would have been but little worthy of commendation had they been content to appear as ordinary human beings, or animals, or even in fancy costume. The

Swiss divine Bullinger, after a lengthy and elaborately learned argument as to the particular day in the week of creation upon which it was most probable that God called the angels into being, says, by way of peroration, "Let us lead a holy and angel-like life in the sight of God's holy angels. Let us watch, lest he that transfigureth and turneth himself into an

angel of light under a good show and likeness deceive us."[1] They even went so far, according to Cranmer,[2] as to appear in the likeness of Christ, in their desire to mislead mankind; for—

"When devils will the blackest sins put on,

They do suggest at first with heavenly shows."[3]

[Footnote 1: Bullinger, Fourth Decade, 9th Sermon. Parker Society.]

[Footnote 2: Cranmer, Confutation, p. 42. Parker Society.]

[Footnote 3: Othello, II. iii. 357. Cf. Love's Labour's Lost, IV. iii. 257; Comedy of Errors, IV. iii. 56.]

55. But one of the most ordinary forms supposed at this period to be assumed by devils was that of a dead friend of the object of the visitation. Before the Reformation, the belief that the spirits of the departed had power at will to revisit the scenes and companions of their earthly life was almost universal. The reforming divines distinctly denied the possibility of such a revisitation, and accounted for the undoubted phenomena, as usual, by attributing them to the devil.[1] James I. says that the devil, when appearing to men, frequently assumed the form of a person newly dead, "to make them believe that it was some good spirit that appeared to them, either to forewarn them of the death of their friend, or else to discover unto them the will of the defunct, or what was the way of his slaughter.... For he dare not so illude anie that knoweth that neither can the spirit of the defunct return to his friend, nor yet an angell use

50

such formes."[2] He further explains that such devils follow mortals to obtain two ends: "the one is the tinsell (loss) of their life by inducing them to such perrilous places at such times as he either follows or possesses them. The other thing that he preases to obtain is the tinsell of their soule."[3]

[Footnote 1: See Hooper's Declaration of the Ten Commandments. Parker Society. Hooper, 326.]

[Footnote 2: Daemonologie, p. 60.]

[Footnote 3: Cf. Hamlet, I. iv. 60-80; and post, § 58.]

56. But the belief in the appearance of ghosts was too deeply rooted in the popular mind to be extirpated, or even greatly affected, by a dogmatic

declaration. The masses went on believing as they always had believed, and as their fathers had believed before them, in spite of the Reformers, and to their no little discontent. Pilkington, Bishop of Durham, in a letter to Archbishop Parker, dated 1564, complains that, "among other things that be amiss here in your great cares, ye shall understand that in Blackburn there is a fantastical (and as some say, lunatic) young man, which says that he has spoken with one of his neighbours that died four year since, or more. Divers times he says he has seen him, and talked with him, and took with him the curate, the schoolmaster, and other neighbours, who all affirm that they see him. *These things be so commonhere* that none in authority will gainsay it, but rather believe and confirm it, that everybody believes it. If I had known how to examine with authority, I would have done it."[1] Here is a little glimpse at the practical troubles of a well-intentioned bishop of the sixteenth century that is surely worth preserving.

[Footnote 1: Parker Correspondence, 222. Parker Society.]

57. There were thus two opposite schools of belief in this matter

of the supposed spirits of the departed:—the conservative, which held to the old doctrine of ghosts; and the reforming, which denied the possibility of ghosts, and held to the theory of devils. In the midst of this disagreement of doctors it was difficult for a plain man to come to a definite conclusion upon the question; and, in consequence, all who were not content with quiet dogmatism were in a state of utter uncertainty upon a point not entirely without importance in practical life as well as in theory. This was probably the position in which the majority of thoughtful men found themselves; and it is accurately reflected in three of Shakspere's plays, which, for other and weightier reasons, are grouped together in the same chronological division—"Julius Caesar,""Macbeth," and "Hamlet."

In the first-mentioned play, Brutus, who afterwards confesses his belief that the apparition he saw at Sardis was the ghost of Caesar,[1] when in the actual presence of the spirit, says—

"Art thou some god, some angel, or some devil?"[2]

The same doubt flashes across the mind of Macbeth on the second entrance of Banquo's ghost—which is probably intended to be a devil appearing at the instigation of the witches—when he says, with evident allusion to a diabolic power before referred to—

"What man dare, I dare:

Approach thou like the rugged Russian bear, The armed rhinoceros, or the Hyrcan tiger,

Take any shape but that."[3]

[Footnote 1: Julius Caesar, V. v. 17.]

[Footnote 2: Ibid. IV. iii. 279.]

[Footnote 3: Macbeth, III. iv. 100.]

52

58. But it is in "Hamlet" that the undecided state of opinion upon this subject is most clearly reflected; and hardly enough influence has been allowed to the doubts arising from this conflict of belief, as urgent or deterrent motives in the play, because this temporary condition of thought has been lost sight of. It is exceedingly interesting to note how frequently the characters who have to do with the apparition of the late King Hamlet alternate between the theories that it is a ghost and that it is a devil which they have seen. The whole subject has such an important bearing upon any attempt to estimate the character of Hamlet, that no excuse need be offered for once again traversing such well-trodden ground.

Horatio, it is true, is introduced to us in a state of determined scepticism; but this lasts for a few seconds only, vanishing upon the first entrance of the spectre, and never again appearing. His first inclination seems to be to the belief that he is the victim of a diabolical illusion; for he says—

"What art thou, that *usurp'st* this time of night, Together with that fair and warlike form

In which the majesty of buried Denmark

Did sometimes march?"[1]

And Marcellus seems to be of the same opinion, for immediately before, he exclaims—

"Thou art a scholar, speak to it, Horatio;"

having apparently the same idea as had Coachman Toby, in "The Night-Walker,"

when he exclaims—

"Let's call the butler up, for he speaks Latin, And that will daunt the devil."[2]

On the second appearance of the illusion, however, Horatio leans to the opinion that it is really the ghost of the late king that he sees, probably in consequence of the conversation that has taken place since the former visitation; and he now appeals to the ghost for information that may enable him to procure rest for his wandering soul. Again, during his interview with Hamlet, when he discloses the secret of the spectre's appearance, though very guarded in his language, Horatio clearly intimates his conviction that he has seen the spirit of the late king.

[Footnote 1: I. i. 46.]

[Footnote 2: II. i.]

The same variation of opinion is visible in Hamlet himself; but, as might be expected, with much more frequent alternations. When first he hears Horatio's story, he seems to incline to the belief that it must be the work of some diabolic agency:

"If it assume my noble father's person,

I'll speak to it, though hell itself should gape, And bid me hold my peace;"[1]

although, characteristically, in almost the next line he exclaims—

"My father's spirit in arms! All is not well," etc.

This, too, seems to be the dominant idea in his mind when he is first brought face to face with the apparition and exclaims—

"Angels and ministers of grace defend us!—

Be thou a spirit of health, or goblin damned,

Bring with thee airs from heaven, or blasts from hell, Be thine intents wicked or charitable,

Thou com'st in such a questionable shape,

That I will speak to thee."[2]

For it cannot be supposed that Hamlet imagined that a "goblin damned" could actually be the spirit of his dead father; and, therefore, the alternative in his mind must have been that he saw a devil assuming his father's likeness—a form which the Evil One knew would most incite Hamlet to intercourse. But even as he speaks, the other theory gradually obtains ascendency in his mind, until it

becomes strong enough to induce him to follow the spirit.

[Footnote 1: I. ii. 244.]

[Footnote 2: I. iv. 39.]

But whilst the devil-theory is gradually relaxing its hold upon Hamlet's mind, it is fastening itself with ever-increasing force upon the minds of his companions; and Horatio expresses their fears in words that are worth comparing with those just quoted from James's "Daemonologie." Hamlet responds to their entreaties not to follow the spectre thus—

"Why, what should be the fear?

I do not set my life at a pin's fee;

And, for my soul, what can it do to that,

Being a thing immortal as itself?"

And Horatio answers—

"What if it tempt you toward the flood, my lord, Or to the dreadful summit of the cliff,

That beetles o'er his base into the sea,

And there assume some other horrible form,

Which might deprive your sovereignty of reason,

And draw you into madness?"

The idea that the devil assumed the form of a dead friend in order to procure the

"tinsell" of both body and soul of his victim is here vividly before the minds of the speakers of these passages.[1]

[Footnote 1: See ante, § 55.]

The subsequent scene with the ghost convinces Hamlet that he is not the victim of malign influences—as far as he is capable of conviction, for his very first words when alone restate the doubt:

"O all you host of heaven! O earth! *What else?* And shall I couple hell?"[1]

and the enthusiasm with which he is inspired in consequence of this interview is

sufficient to support his certainty of conviction until the time for decisive action again arrives. It is not until the idea of the play-test occurs to him that his doubts are once more aroused; and then they return with redoubled force:—

"The spirit that I have seen

May be the devil: and the devil hath power

To assume a pleasing shape; yea, and, perhaps,

Out of my weakness and my melancholy,

(As he is very potent with such spirits,)

Abuses me to damn me."[2]

And he again alludes to this in his speech to Horatio, just before the entry of the king and his train to witness the performance of the players.[3]

[Footnote 1: I. v. 92.]

[Footnote 2: II. ii. 627.]

[Footnote 3: III. ii. 87.]

59. This question was, in Shakspere's time, quite a legitimate element of uncertainty in the complicated problem that presented itself for solution to Hamlet's ever-analyzing mind; and this being so, an apparent inconsistency in detail which has usually been charged upon Shakspere with regard to this play, can be satisfactorily explained. Some critics are never weary of exclaiming that Shakspere's genius was so vast and uncontrollable that it must not be tested, or expected to be found conformable to the rules of art that limit ordinary mortals; that there are many discrepancies and errors in his plays that are to be condoned upon that account; in fact, that he was a very careless and slovenly workman. A favourite instance of this is taken from "Hamlet," where Shakspere actually makes the chief character of the play talk of death as "the bourne from whence no traveller returns" not long after he has been engaged in a prolonged conversation with such a returned traveller.

Now, no artist, however distinguished or however transcendent his genius, is to be pardoned for insincere workmanship, and the greater the man, the less his excuse. Errors arising from want of information (and Shakspere commits these often) may be pardoned if the means for correcting them be unattainable; but errors arising from mere carelessness are not to be pardoned. Further, in many of these cases of supposed contradiction there is an element of carelessness indeed; but it lies at the door of the critic, not of the author; and this appears to be true in the present instance. The dilemma, as it presented itself to the contemporary mind, must be carefully kept in view. Either the spirits of the departed could revisit this world, or they could not. If they could not, then the apparitions mistaken for them must be devils assuming their forms. Now, the tendency of Hamlet's mind, immediately before the great soliloquy on suicide, is decidedly in favour of the latter alternative. The last words that he has uttered, which are also the last quoted here,[1] are those in which he declares most forcibly that he believes the devil-theory possible, and consequently that the dead do not return to this world; and his utterances in his soliloquy are only an accentuate and outcome of this feeling of uncertainty. The very root of his desire for death is that he cannot discard with any feeling of certitude the Protestant doctrine that no traveller does after death return from the invisible world, and that the so-called ghosts are a diabolic deception.

[Footnote 1: § 58, p. 59.]

60. Another power possessed by the evil spirits, and one that excited much attention and created an immense amount of strife during Elizabethan times, was that of entering into the bodies of human beings, or otherwise influencing them so as utterly to deprive them of all self-control, and render them mere automata under the command of the fiends. This was known as possession, or obsession. It was another of the mediaeval beliefs against which the reformers steadily set their faces; and all the resources of their casuistry were exhausted to expose its absurdity. But their position in this respect was an extremely delicate one. On one side of them zealous Catholics were exorcising devils, who shrieked out their testimony to the eternal truth of the Holy Catholic Church; whilst at the same time, on the other side, the zealous Puritans of the extremer sort

were casting out fiends, who bore equally fervent testimony to the superior efficacy and purity of the Protestant faith. The tendency of the more moderate members of the party, therefore was towards a compromise similar to that arrived at upon the question how the devils came by the forms in which they appeared upon the earth. They could not admit that devils could actually enter into and possess the body of a man in those latter days, although during the earlier history of the Church such things had been permitted by Divine Providence for some inscrutable but doubtless satisfactory reason:—that was Catholicism. On the other hand, they could not for an instant tolerate or even sanction the doctrine that devils had no power whatever over humanity:—that was Atheism. But it was quite possible that evil spirits, without actually entering into the body of aman, might so infest, worry, and torment him, as to produce all the symptoms indicative of possession. The doctrine of obsession replaced that of possession; and, once adopted, was supported by a string of those quaint, conceited arguments so peculiar to the time.[1]

[Footnote 1: Dialogicall Discourses, by Deacon and Walker, 3rd Dialogue.]

61. But, as in all other cases, the refinements of the theologians had little or no effect upon the world outside their controversies. To the ordinary mind, if a man's eyes goggled, body swelled, and mouth foamed, and it was admitted that these were the work of a devil, the question whether the evil-doer were actually housed within the sufferer, or only hovered in his immediate neighbourhood, seemed a question of such minor importance as to be hardly worth discussing—a conclusion that the lay mind is apt to come to upon other questions that appear portentous to the divines—and the theory of possession, having the advantage in time over that of obsession, was hard to dislodge.

62. One of the chief causes of the persistency with which the old belief was maintained was the utter ignorance of the medical men of the period on the subject of mental disease. The doctors of the time were mere children in knowledge of the science they professed; and to attribute a disease, the symptoms of which they could not comprehend, to a power

outside their control by ordinary methods, was a safe method of screening a reputation which might otherwise have suffered. "Canst thou not minister to a mind diseased?" cries Macbeth to the doctor, in one of those moments of yearning after the better life he regrets, but cannot return to, which come over him now and again. No; the disease is beyond his practice; and, although this passage has in it a deeper meaning than the one attributed to it here, it well illustrates the position of the medical man in such cases. Most doctors of the time were mere empirics; dabbled more or less in alchemy; and, in the treatment of mental disease, were little better than children. They had for co-practitioners all who, by their credit with the populace for superior wisdom, found themselves in a position to engage in a profitable employment. Priests, preachers, schoolmasters—Dr. Pinches and Sir Topazes—became so commonly exorcists, that the Church found it necessary to forbid the casting out of spirits without a special license for that purpose.[1]

But as the Reformers only combated the doctrine of possession upon strictly theological grounds, and did not go on to suggest any substitute for the time-honoured practice of exorcism as a means for getting rid of the admittedly

obnoxious result of diabolic interference, it is not altogether surprising that the method of treatment did not immediately change.

[Footnote 1: 72nd Canon.]

63. Upon this subject a book called "Tryal of Witchcraft," by John Cotta,

"Doctor in Physike," published in 1616, is extremely instructive. The writer is evidently in advance of his time in his opinions upon the principal subject with which he professes to deal, and weighs the evidence for and against the reality of witchcraft with extreme precision and fairness. In the course of his argument he has to distinguish the symptoms that show a person to have been bewitched, from those that point to a demoniacal possession.[1] "Reason doth detect," says he, "the sicke to be afflicted by the immediate supernaturall power of the devil two wayes: the first way is by such things as are subject and manifest to the learned physicion only; the second is by such things as are subject and manifest to the vulgar view." The two signs by which the "learned physicion" recognized diabolic intervention were: first, the preternatural appearance of the disease from which the patient was suffering; and, secondly, the inefficacy of the remedies applied. In other words, if the leech encountered any disease the symptoms of which were unknown to him, or if, through some unforeseen circumstances, the drug he prescribed failed to operate in its accustomed manner, a case of demoniacal possession was considered to be conclusively proved, and the medical man was merged in the magician.

[Footnote 1: Ch. 10.]

64. The second class of cases, in which the diabolic agency is palpable to the layman as well as the doctor, Cotta illustrates thus: "In the time of their paroxysmes or fits, some diseased persons have been seene to vomit crooked iron, coales, brimstone, nailes, needles, pinnes, lumps of lead, waxe, hayre, strawe, and the like, in such quantities, figure, fashion, and proportion as could never possiblie pass down, or arise up thorow the natural narrownesse of the throate, or be contained in the unproportionable small capacitie, naturall susceptibilitie, and position of the stomake." Possessed persons, he says, were also clairvoyant, telling what was being said and done at a far distance; and also spoke languages which at ordinary times they did not understand, as their successors, the modern spirit mediums, do. This gift of tongues was one of the prominent features of the possession of Will Sommers and the other persons exorcised by the Protestant preacher John Darrell, whose performances as an

exorcist created quite a domestic sensation in England at the close of the sixteenth century.[1] The whole affair was investigated by Dr. Harsnet, who had already acquired fame as an iconoclast in these matters, as will presently be seen; but it would have little more than an antiquarian interest now, were it not for the fact that Ben Jonson made it the subject of his satire in one of his most humorous plays, "The Devil is an Ass." In it he turns the last-mentioned peculiarity to good account; for when Fitzdottrell, in the fifth act, feigns madness, and quotes Aristophanes, and speaks in Spanish and French, the judicious Sir Paul Eithersides comes to the conclusion that "it is the devil by his several languages."

[Footnote 1: A True Relation of the Grievious Handling of William Sommers, etc. London: T. Harper, 1641 (? 1601). The Tryall of Maister Darrell, 1599.]

65. But more interesting, and more important for the present purpose, are the cases of possession that were dealt with by Father Parsons and his colleagues in 1585-6, and of which Dr. Harsnet gave such a highly spiced and entertaining account in his "Declaration of Egregious Popish Impostures," first published in the year 1603. It is from this work that Shakspere took the names of the devils mentioned by Edgar, and other references made by him in "King Lear;" and an outline of the relation of the play to the book will furnish incidentally much matter illustrative of the subject of possession. But before entering upon this outline, a brief glance at the condition of affairs political and domestic, which partially caused and nourished these extraordinary eccentricities, is almost essential to a proper understanding of them.

66. The year 1586 was probably one of the most critical years that England has passed through since she was first a nation. Standing alone amongst the European States, with even the Netherlanders growing cold towards her on account of her ambiguous treatment of them, she had to fight out the battle of her independence against odds to all appearances irresistible. With Sixtus plotting her overthrow at Rome, Philip at Madrid, Mendoza and the English traitors at Paris, and Mary of Scotland at Chartley, while a third of her people were malcontent, and James the Sixth was friend or enemy as it best suited his convenience, the outlook was anything but reassuring for the brave men who held the helm in those stormy times. But although England owed her deliverance chiefly to the forethought and hardihood of her sons, it cannot be doubted that the sheer imbecility of her foes contributed not a little to that result. To boththese

conditions she owed the fact that the great Armada, the embodiment of the foreign hatred and hostility, threatening to break upon her shores like a huge wave, vanished like its spray. Medina Sidonia, with his querulous complaints and general ineffectuality,[1] was hardly a match for Drake and his sturdy companions; nor were the leaders of the Babington conspiracy, the representatives and would-be leaders of the corresponding internal convulsion, the infatuated worshippers of the fair devil of Scotland, the men to cope for a moment with the intellects of Walsingham and Burleigh.

[Footnote 1: Froude, xii. p. 405.]

67. The events which Harsnet investigated and wrote upon with politico-theological animus formed an eddy in the main current of the Babington conspiracy. For some years before that plot had taken definite shape, seminary priests had been swarming into England from the continent, and were sedulously engaged in preaching rebellion in the rural districts, sheltered and protected by the more powerful of the disaffected nobles and gentry—modern apostles, preparing the way before the future regenerator of England, Cardinal Allen, the would-be Catholic Archbishop of Canterbury. Among these was one Weston, who, in his enthusiastic admiration for the martyr-traitor, Edmund Campion, had adopted the alias of Edmonds. This Jesuit was gifted with the power of casting out devils, and he exercised it in order to prove the divine origin of the Holy Catholic faith, and, by implication, the duty of all persons religiously inclined, to rebel against a sovereign who was ruthlessly treading it into the dust. The performances which Harsnet examined into took place chiefly in the house of Lord Vaux at Hackney, and of one Peckham at Denham, in the end of the year 1585 and the beginning of 1586. The possessed persons were Anthony Tyrell, another Jesuit who rounded upon his friends in the time of their tribulation;[1]

Marwood, Antony Babington's private servant, who subsequently found it convenient to leave the country, and was never examined upon the subject; Trayford and Mainy, two young gentlemen, and Sara and Friswood Williams, and Anne Smith, maid-servants. Richard Mainy, the most edifying subject of them all, was seventeen only when the possession seized him; he had only just returned to England from Rheims, and, when passing through Paris, had come under the influence of Charles Paget and Morgan; so his antecedents appeared somewhat open to suspicion.[2]

[Footnote 1: The Fall of Anthony Tyrell, by Persoun. See The Troubles of our Catholic Forefathers, by John Morris, p. 103.]

[Footnote 2: He was examined by the Government as to his connection with the Paris conspirators.—See State Papers, vol. clxxx. 16, 17.]

68. With the truth or falsehood of the statements and deductions made by Harsnet, we have little or no concern. Western did not pretend to deny that he had the power of exorcism, or that he exercised it upon the persons in question, but he did not admit the truth of any of the more ridiculous stories which Harsnet so triumphantly brings forward to convict him of intentional deceit; and his features, if the portrait in Father Morris's book is an accurate representation of him, convey an impression of feeble, unpractical piety that one is loth to associate with a malicious impostor. In addition to this, one of the witnesses against him, Tyrell, was a manifest knave and coward; another, Mainy, as conspicuous a fool; while the rest were servant-maids—all of them interested in exonerating themselves from the stigma of having been adherents of a lost cause, at the expense of a ringleader who seemed to have made himself too conspicuous to escape punishment. Furthermore, the evidence of these witnesses was not taken until 1598 and 1602, twelve and sixteen years after the events to which it related took place; and when taken, was taken by Harsnet, a violent Protestant and almost maniacal exorcist-hunter, as the miscellaneous collection of literature evoked by his exposure of Parson Darrell's dealings with Will Sommers and others will show.

69. Among the many devils' names mentioned by Harsnet in his "Declaration,"

and in the examinations of witnesses annexed to it, the following have undoubtedly been repeated in "King Lear":—Fliberdigibet, spelt in the play Flibbertigibbet; Hoberdidance called Hopdance and Hobbididance; and Frateretto, who are called morris-dancers; Haberdicut, who appears in "Lear" as Obidicut; Smolkin, one of Trayford's devils; Modu, who possessed Mainy; and Maho, who possessed Sara Williams. These two latter devils have in the play managed to exchange the final vowels of their names, and appear as Modo and Mahu.[1]

[Footnote 1: In addition to these, Killico has probably been corrupted into Pillicock—a much more probable explanation of the word than either of those suggested by Dyce in his glossary; and I have little doubt that the ordinary reading of the line, "Pur! the cat is gray!" in Act III. vi. 47, is incorrect; that Pur is not an interjection, but the repetition of the name of another devil, Purre, who is mentioned by Harsnet. The passage in question occurs only in the quartos, and therefore the fact that there is no stop at all after the word "Pur" cannot be reliedupon as helping to prove the correctness of this supposition. On the other hand, there is nothing in the texts to justify the insertion of the note of exclamation.]

70. A comparison of the passages in "King Lear" spoken by Edgar when feigning madness, with those in Harsnet's book which seem to have suggested them, will furnish as vivid a picture as it is possible to give of the state of contemporary belief upon the subject of possession. It is impossible not to notice that nearly all the allusions in the play refer to the performance of the youth Richard Mainy. Even Edgar's hypothetical account of his moral failings in the past seems to have been an accurate reproduction of Mainy's conduct in some particulars, as the quotation below will prove;[1] and there appears to be so little necessity for these remarks of Edgar's, that it seems almost possible that there may have been some point in these passages that has since been lost. A careful search, however, has failed to disclose any reason why Mainy should be held up to obloquy; and the passages in question were evidently not the result of a direct reference to the "Declaration." After his examination by Harsnet in 1602, Mainy seems to have sunk into the insignificant position which he was so calculated to adorn, and nothing more is heard of him;

so the references to him must be accidental merely.

[Footnote 1: "He would needs have persuaded this examinate's sister to have gone thence with him in the apparel of a youth, and to have been his boy and waited upon him.... He urged this examinate divers times to have yielded to his carnal desires, using very unfit tricks with her. There was also a very proper woman, one Mistress Plater, with whom this examinate perceived he had many allurements, showing great tokens of extraordinary affection towards her."—

Evidence of Sara Williams, Harsnet, p. 190. Compare King Lear, Act iii. sc. iv.

ll. 82-101; note especially l. 84.]

71. One curious little repetition in the play of a somewhat unimportant incident recorded by Harsnet is to be found in the fourth scene of the third act, where Edgar says—

"Who gives anything to poor Tom? whom the foul fiend hath led through fire and through flame, and through ford and whirlpool, o'er bog and quagmire; *thathath laid knives under his pillow, and halters in his pew*; set ratsbane by his porridge," etc.[1]

[Footnote 1: l. 51, et seq.]

The events referred to took place at Denham. A halter and some knife-blades were found in a corridor of the house. "A great search was made in the house to know how the said halter and knife-blades came thither, but it could not in any wise be found out, as it was pretended, till Master Mainy in his next fit said, as it was reported, that the devil layd them in the gallery, that some of those that were possessed might either hang themselves with the halter, or kill themselves with the blades."[1]

[Footnote 1: Harsnet, p. 218.]

72. But the bulk of the references relating to the possession of Mainy occur further on in the same scene:—

"*Fool.* This cold night will turn us all to fools and madmen.

"*Edgar.* Take heed o' the foul fiend: obey thy parents; keep thy word justly; swear not; commit not with man's sworn spouse;[1] set not thy sweet heart on proud array: Tom's a-cold.

"*Lear.* What hast thou been?

"*Edgar.* A serving-man, proud in heart and mind, that curled my hair, wore my gloves in my cap, served the lust of my mistress' heart, and did the act of darkness with her;[2] swore as many oaths as I spake words, and broke them in the sweet face of heaven; one that slept in the contriving of lust, and waked to do it; wine loved I deeply; dice dearly; and in women out-paramoured the Turk: false of heart, light of ear, bloody of hand; hog in sloth, fox in stealth, wolf in greediness, dog in madness, lion in prey. Let not the creaking of shoes, nor the rustling of silks, betray thy poor heart to woman; keep thy foot out of brothels, thy hand out of plackets,[3] thy pen from lenders' books, and defy the foul fiend."[4]

[Footnote 1: Cf. § 70, and note.]

[Footnote 2: Cf. § 70, and note.]

[Footnote 3: Placket probably here means pockets; not, as usual, the slip in a petticoat. Tom was possessed by Mahu, the prince of stealing.]

[Footnote 4: l. 82, et seq.]

This must be read in conjunction with what Edgar says of himself subsequently:

"Five fiends have been in poor Tom at once; of lust, as Obidicut; Hobbididance, prince of dumbness; Mahu, of stealing; Modo, of murder; Flibbertigibbet, of mopping and mowing; who since possesses chamber-maids and waiting-women."[1]

[Footnote 1: Act IV. i. 61.]

The following are the chief parts of the account given by Harsnet of the exorcism of Mainy by Weston—a most extraordinary transaction, —said to be taken from Weston's own account of the matter. He was supposed to be possessed by the devils who represented the seven deadly sins, and "by instigation of the first of the seven, began to set his hands into his side, curled his hair, and used such gestures as Maister Edmunds present affirmed that that spirit was Pride.[1] Heerewith he began to curse and to banne, saying, 'What a poxe do I heare? I will stay no longer among a company of rascal priests, but goe to the court and brave it amongst my fellowes, the noblemen there assembled.'[2] ...

Then Maister Edmunds did proceede againe with his exorcismes, and suddenly the sences of Mainy were taken from him, his belly began to swell, and his eyes to stare, and suddainly he cried out, 'Ten pounds in the hundred!' he called for a scrivener to make a bond, swearing that he would not lend his money without a pawne.... There could be no other talke had with this spirit but money and usury, so as all the company deemed this devil to be the author of Covetousnesse....[3]

[Footnote 1: "A serving-man, proud of heart and mind, that curled my hair," etc.

—l. 87; cf. also l. 84. Curling the hair as a sign of Mainy's possession is mentioned again, Harsnet, p. 57.]

[Footnote 2: "That ... swore as many oaths as I spake words, and broke them in the sweet face of heaven."—l. 90.]

[Footnote 3: "Keep ... thy pen out of lenders' books."—l. 100.]

"Ere long Maister Edmunds beginneth againe his exorcismes, wherein he had not proceeded farre, but up cometh another spirit singing most filthy and baudy songs: every word almost that he spake was nothing but ribaldry. They that were present with one voyce affirmed that devill to be the author of Luxury.[1]

[Footnote 1: "Wine loved I deeply; dice dearly; and in women out-paramoured the Turk."—l. 93.]

"Envy was described by disdainful looks and contemptuous speeches; Wrath, by furious gestures, and talke as though he would have fought;[1]

Gluttony, by vomiting;[2] and Sloth,[3] by gasping and snorting, as though he had been asleepe."[4]

[Footnote 1: "Dog in madness, lion in prey."—l. 96.]

[Footnote 2: "Wolf in greediness."—Ibid.]

[Footnote 3: "Hog in sloth."—l. 95.]

[Footnote 4: Harsnet, p. 278.]

A sort of prayer-meeting was then held for the relief of the distressed youth:

"Whereupon the spirit of Pride departed in the forme of a Peacocke; the spirit of Sloth in the likenesse of an Asse; the spirit of Envy in the similitude of a Dog; the spirit of Gluttony in the forme of a Wolfe."[1]

[Footnote 1: The words, "Hog in sloth, fox in stealth, wolf in greediness, dog in madness, lion in prey," are clearly an imperfect reminiscence of this part of the transaction.]

There is in another part of "King Lear" a further reference to the incidents attendant upon these exorcisms Edgar says,[1] "The foul fiend haunts poor Tom in the voice of a nightingale." This seems to refer to the following incident related by Friswood Williams:—

"There was also another strange thing happened at Denham about a bird. Mistris Peckham had a nightingale, which she kept in a cage, wherein Maister Dibdale took great delight, and would often be playing with it. This nightingale was one night conveyed out of the cage, and being next morning diligently sought for, could not be heard of, till Maister Mainie's devil, in one of his fits (as it was pretended), said that the wicked spirit which was in this examinate's sister[2] had taken the bird out of the cage, and killed it in despite of Maister Dibdale."[3]

[Footnote 1: Act III. sc. vi. l. 31.]

[Footnote 2: Sara Williams.]

[Footnote 3: Harsnet, p. 225.]

73. The treatment to which, in consequence of his belief in possession, unfortunate persons like Mainy and Sommers, who were probably only suffering from some harmless form of mental disease, were subjected, was hardly calculated to effect a cure. The most ignorant quack was considered perfectly competent to deal with cases which, in reality, require the most delicate and judicious management, combined with the profoundest physiological, as well as psychological, knowledge. The ordinary method of dealing with these lunatics was as simple as it was irritating. Bonds and confinement in a darkened room were the specifics; and the monotony of this treatment was relieved by occasional visits from the sage who had charge of the case, to mumble a prayer or mutter an exorcism. Another popular but unpleasant cure was by flagellation; so that Romeo's

"Not mad, but bound more than a madman is,

Shut up in prison, kept without my food,

Whipped and tormented,"[1]

if an exaggerated description of his own mental condition is in itself no inflated metaphor.

[Footnote 1: I. ii. 55.]

74. Shakspere, in "The Comedy of Errors," and indirectly also in "Twelfth Night," has given us intentionally ridiculous illustrations of scenes which he had not improbably witnessed, in the country at any rate, and which bring vividly before us the absurdity of the methods of diagnosis and treatment usually adopted:—

Courtesan. How say you now? is not your husband mad?

Adriana. His incivility confirms no less.

Good doctor Pinch, you are a conjurer;

Establish him in his true sense again,

And I will please you what you will demand.

Luciana. Alas! how fiery and how sharp he looks!

Courtesan. Mark how he trembles in his extasy!

Pinch. Give me your hand, and let me feel your pulse.[1]

Ant. E. There is my hand, and let it feel your ear.

Pinch. I charge thee, Satan, housed within this man, To yield possession to my holy prayers,

And to thy state of darkness his thee straight;

I conjure thee by all the saints in heaven.

Ant. E. Peace, doting wizard, peace; I am not mad.

Pinch. O that thou wert not, poor distressed soul![2]

After some further business, Pinch pronounces his opinion:

"Mistress, both man and master are possessed; I know it by their pale and deadly looks:

They must be bound, and laid in some dark room."[3]

But "good doctor Pinch" seems to have been mild even to feebleness in his conjuration; many of his brethren in art had much more effective formulae. It seems that devils were peculiarly sensitive to any opprobrious epithets that chanced to be bestowed upon them. The skilful exorcist took advantage of this weakness, and, if he could only manage to keep up a flow of uncomplimentary remarks sufficiently long and offensive, the unfortunate spirit became embarrassed, restless, agitated, and finally took to flight. Here is a specimen of the "nicknames" which had so potent an effect, if Harsnet is to be credited:—

"Heare therefore, thou senceless false lewd spirit, maister of devils, miserable creature, tempter of men, deceaver of bad angels, captaine of heretiques, father of lyes, fatuous bestial ninnie, drunkard, infernal theefe, wicked serpent, ravening woolfe, leane hunger-bitten impure sow, seely beast, truculent beast, cruel beast, bloody beast, beast of all blasts, the most bestiall acherontall spirit, smoakie spirit, Tartareus spirit!"[4] Whether this objurgation terminates from loss of breath on the part of the conjurer, or the precipitate departure of the spirit addressed, it is impossible to say; it is difficult to imagine any logical reason for its conclusion.

[Footnote 1: The cessation of the pulse was one of the symptoms of possession.

See the case of Sommers, Tryal of Maister Darrell, 1599.]

[Footnote 2: IV. iv. 48, 62.]

[Footnote 3: Ibid. 95.]

[Footnote 4: Harsnet, p. 113.]

75. Occasionally other, and sometimes more elaborate, methods of exorcism than those mentioned by Romeo were adopted, especially when the operation was conducted for the purpose of bringing into prominence some great religious truth. The more evangelical of the operators adopted the plan of lying on the top of their patients, "after the manner of Elias and Pawle."[1] But the Catholic exorcists invented and carried to perfection the greatest refinement in the art.

The patient, seated in a "holy chair," specially sanctified for the occasion, was compelled to drink about a pint of a compound of sack and salad oil; after which refreshment a pan of burning brimstone was held under his nose, until his face was blackened by the smoke.[2] All this while the officiating priest kept up his invocation of the fiends in the manner illustrated above; and, under such circumstances, it is extremely doubtful whether the most determined character would not be prepared to see somewhat unusual phenomena for the sake of a short respite.

[Footnote 1: The Tryall of Maister Darrell, 1599, p. 2.]

[Footnote 2: Harsnet, p. 53.]

76. Another remarkable method of exorcism was a process termed "firing out"

the fiend.[1] The holy flame of piety resident in the priest was so terrible to the evil spirit, that the mere contact of the holy hand with that part of the body of the afflicted person in which he was resident was enough to make him shrink away into some more distant portion; so, by a judicious application of the hand, the exorcist could drive the devil into some limb, from which escape into the body was impossible, and the evil spirit, driven to the extremity, was obliged to depart, defeated and disgraced.[2] This influence could be exerted, however, without actual corporal contact, as the following quaint extract from Harsnet's book will show:—

"Some punie rash devil doth stay till the holy priest be come somewhat neare, as

into the chamber where the demoniacke doth abide, purposing, as it seemes, to try a pluck with the priest; and then his hart sodainly failing him (as Demas, when he saw his friend Chinias approach), cries out that he is tormented with the presence of the priest, and so is fierd out of his hold."[3]

[Footnote 1: This expression occurs in Sonnet cxliv., and evidently with the meaning here explained; only the bad angel is supposed to fire out the good one.]

[Footnote 2: Harsnet, pp. 77, 96, 97.]

[Footnote 3: Ibid. p. 65.]

77. The more violent or uncommon of the bodily diseases were, as the quotation from Cotta's book shows[1], attributed to the same diabolic source. In an era when the most profound ignorance prevailed with regard to the simplest laws of health; when the commoner diseases were considered as God's punishment for sin, and not attributable to natural causes; when so eminent a divine as Bishop Hooper could declare that "the air, the water, and the earth have no poison in themselves to hurt their lord and master man,"[2] unless man first poisoned himself with sin;

and when, in consequence of this ignorance and this false philosophy, and the inevitable neglect attendant upon them, those fearful plagues known as "the Black Death" could, almost without notice, sweep down upon a country, and decimate its inhabitants—it is not wonderful that these terrible scourges were attributed to the malevolence of the Evil One.

[Footnote 1: See §§ 63, 64.]

[Footnote 2: I Hooper, p. 308. Parker Society.]

78. But it is curious to notice that, although possessing such terrible powers over the bodies and minds of mortals, devils were not believed to be potent enough to destroy the lives of the persons they persecuted unless they could persuade their victims to renounce God. This theory probably sprang out of the limitation imposed by the Almighty upon the power of Satan during his temptation of Job, and the advice given to the sufferer by his wife, "Curse God, and die." Hence, when evil spirits began their assaults upon a man, one of their first endeavours was to induce him to do some act that would be equivalent to such a renunciation. Sometimes this was a bond assigning the victim's soul to the Evil One in consideration of certain worldly advantages; sometimes a formal denialof his baptism; sometimes a deed that drives away the guardian angel from his side, and leaves the devil's influence uncounteracted. In "The Witch of Edmonton,"[1] the first act that Mother Sawyer demands her familiar to perform after she has struck her bargain, is to kill her enemy Banks; and the fiend has reluctantly to declare that he cannot do so unless by good fortune he could happen to catch him cursing. Both Harpax[2] and Mephistophiles[3] suggest to their victims that they have power to destroy their enemies, but neither of them is able to exercise it. Faust can torment, but not kill, his would-be murderers; and Springius and Hircius are powerless to take Dorothea's life. In the latter case it is distinctly the protection of the guardian angel that limits the diabolic power; so it is not unnatural that Gratiano should think the cursing of his better angel from his side the "most desperate turn" that poor old Brabantio could have done himself, had he been living to hear

of his daughter's cruel death.[4] It is next to impossible for people in the present day to have any idea what a consolation this belief in a good attendant spirit, specially appointed to guard weak mortals through life, to ward off evils, and guide to eternal safety, must have been in a time when, according to the current belief, any person, however blameless, however holy, was liable at any moment to be possessed by a devil, or harried and tortured by a witch.

[Footnote 1: Act II. sc. i.]

[Footnote 2: The Virgin Martyr, Act III. sc. iii.]

[Footnote 3: Dr. Faustus, Act I. sc. iii.]

[Footnote 4: Othello, Act V. sc. ii. 204.]

79. This leads by a natural sequence to the consideration of another and more insidious form of attack upon mankind adopted by the evil spirits. Possession and obsession were methods of assault adopted against the will of the afflicted person, and hardly to be avoided by him without the supernatural intervention of the Church. The practice of witchcraft and magic involved the absolute and voluntary barter of body and soul to the Evil One, for the purpose of obtaining a few short years of superhuman power, to be employed for the gratification of the culprit's avarice, ambition, or desire for revenge.

80. In the strange history of that most inexplicable mental disease, the witchcraft epidemic, as it has been justly called by a high authority on such matters,[1] we moderns are, by the nature of our education and prejudices, completely incapacitated for sympathizing with either the persecutors or their victims. We are at a loss to understand how clear-sighted and upright men, like Sir Matthew Hale, could consent to become parties to a relentless persecution to the death of poor helpless beings whose chief crime, in most cases, was, that they had suffered starvation both in body and in mind. We cannot understand it, because none of us believe in the existence of evil spirits. None; for although there are still a

few persons who nominally hold to the ancient faith, as they do to many other respectable but effete traditions, yet they would be at a loss for a reason for the faith that is in them, should they chance to be asked for one; and not one of them would be prepared to make the smallest material sacrifice for the sake of it.

It is true that the existence of evil spirits recently received a tardy and somewhat hesitating recognition in our ecclesiastical courts,[2] which at first authoritatively declared that a denial of the existence of the personality of the devil constituted a man a notorious evil liver, and depraver of the Book of Common Prayer;[3] but this was promptly reversed by the Judicial Committee of the Privy Council, under the auspices of two Low Church law lords and two archbishops, with the very vague proviso that "they do not mean to decide that those doctrines are otherwise than inconsistent with the formularities of the Church of England;"[4] yet the very contempt with which these portentous declarations of Church law have been received shows how great has been the fall of the once almost omnipotent minister of evil. The ancient Satan does indeed exist in some few formularies, but in such a washed-out and flimsy condition as to be the reverse of conspicuous. All that remains of him and of his subordinate legions is the ineffectual ghost of a departed creed, for the resuscitation of which no man will move a finger.

[Footnote 1: See Dr. Carpenter in *Frazer* for November, 1877.]

[Footnote 2: See Jenkins v. Cooke, Law Reports, Admiralty and Ecclesiastical Cases, vol. iv. p. 463, et seq.]

[Footnote 3: Ibid. p. 499, Sir R. Phillimore.]

[Footnote 4: Law Reports, I Probate Division, p. 102.]

81. It is perfectly impossible for us, therefore, to comprehend, although by an effort we may perhaps bring ourselves to imagine, the horror and loathing with which good men, entirely believing in the existence and omnipresence of countless legions of evil spirits, able and

anxious to perpetrate the mischiefs that it has been the object of these pages in some part to describe, would regard those who, for their own selfish gratification, deliberately surrendered their hopes of eternal happiness in exchange for an alliance with the devils, which would render these ten times more capable than before of working their wicked wills.

To men believing this, no punishment could seem too sudden or too terrible for such offenders against religion and society, and no means of possible detection too slight or far-fetched to be neglected; indeed, it might reasonably appear to them better that many innocent persons should perish, with the assurance of future reward for their undeserved sufferings, than that a single guilty one should escape undetected, and become the medium by which the devil might destroy more souls.

82. But the persecuted, far more than the persecutors, deserve our sympathy, although they rarely obtain it. It is frequently asserted that the absolute truth of a doctrine is the only support that will enable its adherents successfully to weather the storms of persecution. Those who assent to this proposition must be prepared to find a large amount of truth in the beliefs known to us under the name of witchcraft, if the position is to be successfully maintained; for never was any sect persecuted more systematically, or with more relentlessness, than these little-offending heretics. Protestants and Catholics, Anglicans and Calvinists, so ready at all times to commit one another to the flames and to the headsman, found in this matter common ground, upon which all could heartily unite for the grand purpose of extirpating error. When, out of the quiet of our own times, we look back upon the terrors of the Tower, and the smoke and glare of Smithfield, we think with mingled pity and admiration of those brave men and women who, in the sixteenth century, enriched with their blood and ashes the soil from whence was to spring our political and religious freedom. But no whit of admiration, hardly a glimmer of pity, is even casually evinced for those poor creatures who, neglected, despised, and abhorred, were, at the same time, dying the same agonizing death, and passing through the torment of the flames to that

"something after death—the undiscovered country," without the sweet assurance which sustained their better-remembered fellow-sufferers, that beyond the martyr's cross was waiting the martyr's crown. No such hope supported those who were condemned to die for the crime of witchcraft: their anticipations of the future were as dreary as their memories of the past, and no friendly voice was raised, or hand stretched out, to encourage or console them during that last sad journey. Their hope of mercy from man was small—strangulation before the application of the fire, instead of the more lingering and painful death at most;—their hope of mercy from Heaven, nothing; yet, under these circumstances, the most auspicious perhaps that could be imagined for the extirpation of a heretical belief, persecution failed to effect its object. The more the Government burnt the witches, the more the crime of witchcraft spread; and it was not until an attitude of contemptuous toleration was adopted towards the culprits that the belief died down, gradually but surely, not on account of the conclusiveness of the arguments directed against it, but from its own inherent lack of vitality.[1]

[Footnote 1: See Mr. Lecky's elaborate and interesting description of the demise of the belief in the first chapter of his History of the Rise of Rationalism in Europe.]

83. The history and phenomena of witchcraft have been so admirably treated by more than one modern investigator, as to render it unnecessary to deal exhaustively with a subject which presents such a vast amount of material for arrangement and comment. The scope of the following remarks will therefore be limited to a consideration of such features of the subject as appear to throw light upon the supernaturalism in "Macbeth." This consideration will be carried out with some minuteness, as certain modern critics, importing mythological learning that is the outcome of comparatively recent investigation into the interpretation of the text, have declared that the three sisters who play such an important part in that drama are not witches at all, but are, or are intimately allied to, the Norns or Fates of Scandinavian paganism. It will be the object of the following pages to illustrate the contemporary belief concerning witches and their powers, by showing that nearly every

characteristic point attributed to the sisters has its counterpart in contemporary witch-lore; that some of the allusions, indeed, bear so strong a resemblance to certain events that had transpired not many years before "Macbeth" was written, that it is not improbable that Shakspere was alluding to them in much the same off-hand, cursory manner as he did to the Mainy incident when writing "King Lear."

84. The first critic whose comments upon this subject call for notice is the eminent Gervinus. In evident ignorance of the history of witchcraft, he says, "In the witches Shakspere has made use of the popular belief in evil geniuses and in adverse persecutors of mankind, and has produced a similar but darker race of beings, just as he made use of the belief in fairies in the 'Midsummer Night's Dream.' This creation is less attractive and complete, but not less masterly. The poet, in the text of the play itself, calls these beings witches only derogatorily; they call themselves weird sisters; the Fates bore this denomination, and the sisters remind us indeed of the Northern Fates or Valkyries. They appear wild and weather-beaten in exterior and attire, common in speech, ignoble, half-human creatures, ugly as the Evil One, and in like manner old, and of neither sex. They are guided by more powerful masters, their work entirely springs from delight in evil, and they are wholly devoid of human sympathies.... They are simply the embodiment of inward temptation; they come in storm and vanish in air, like corporeal impulses, which, originating in the blood, cast up bubbles of sin and ambition in the soul; they are weird sisters only in the sense in which men carry their own fates within their bosoms."[1] This criticism is so entirely subjective and unsupported by evidence that it is difficult to deal satisfactorily with it. It will be shown hereafter that this description does not apply in the least to the Scandinavian Norns, while, so far as it is true to Shakspere's text, it does not clash with contemporary records of the appearance and actions of witches.

[Footnote 1: Shakspere Commentaries, translated by F.E. Bunnert, p. 591.]

85. The next writer to bring forward a view of this character was

the Rev. F.G.

Fleay, the well-known Shakspere critic, whose ingenious efforts in iconoclasm cause a curious alternation of feeling between admiration and amazement. His argument is unfortunately mixed up with a question of textual criticism; for he rejects certain scenes in the play as the work of the inferior dramatist Middleton.

[1] The question relating to the text will only be noticed so far as it is inextricably involved with the argument respecting the nature of the weird sisters. Mr. Fleay's position is, shortly, this. He thinks that Shakspere's play commenced with the entrance of Macbeth and Banquo in the third scene of the first act, and that the weird sisters who subsequently take part in that scene are

Norns, not witches; and that in the first scene of the fourth act, Shakspere discarded the Norns, and introduced three entirely new characters, who were intended to be genuine witches.

[Footnote 1: Of the witch scenes Mr. Fleay rejects Act I. sc. i., and sc. iii. down to l. 37, and Act III. sc. v.]

86. The evidence which can be produced in support of this theory, apart from question of style and probability, is threefold. The first proof is derived from a manuscript entitled "The Booke of Plaies and Notes thereof, for Common Pollicie," written by a somewhat famous magician-doctor, Simon Forman, who was implicated in the murder of Sir Thomas Overbury. He says, "In 'Macbeth,' at the Globe, 1610, the 20th April, Saturday, there was to be observed first how Macbeth and Banquo, two noblemen of Scotland, riding through a wood, there stood before them three women fairies, or nymphs, and saluted Macbeth, saying three times unto him, 'Hail, Macbeth, King of Codor, for thou shalt be a king, but thou shalt beget no kings,'" etc.[1] This, if Forman's account held together decently in other respects, would be strong, although not conclusive, evidence in favour of the theory; but the whole note is so full of inconsistencies and misstatements, that it is not unfair to conclude,

either that the writer was not paying marvellous attention to the entertainment he professed to describe, or that the player's copy differed in many essential points from the present text. Not the least conspicuous of these inconsistencies is the account of the sisters' greeting of Macbeth just quoted. Subsequently Forman narrates that Duncan created Macbeth Prince of Cumberland; and that "when Macbeth had murdered the king, the blood on his hands could not be washed off by any means, nor from his wife's hands, which handled the bloody daggers in hiding them, by which means they became both much amazed and affronted." Such a loose narration cannot be relied upon if the text in question contains any evidence at all rebutting the conclusion that the sisters are intended to be "women fairies, or nymphs."

[Footnote 1: See Furness, Variorum, p. 384.]

87. The second piece of evidence is the story of Macbeth as it is narrated by Holinshed, from which Shakspere derived his material. In that account we read that "It fortuned as Makbeth and Banquho journied toward Fores, where the king then laie, they went sporting by the waie togither without other companie, saue onlie themselues, passing thorough the woods and fields, when suddenlie in the middest of a laund there met them three women in strange and wild apparell, resembling creatures of elder world, whome when they attentivelie beheld, woondering much at the sight, the first of them spake and said; 'All haile, Makbeth, thane of Glammis' (for he had latelie entered into that dignitie and office by the death of his father Sinell). The second of them said; 'Haile, Makbeth, thane of Cawder.' But the third said; 'All haile, Makbeth, that heereafter shall be King of Scotland.' ... Afterwards the common opinion was that these women were either the weird sisters, that is (as ye would say) the goddesses of destinie, or else some nymphs or feiries, indued with knowledge of prophesie by their necromanticall science, because everiething came to passe as they had spoken."[1] This is all that is heard of these "goddesses of Destinie" in Holinshed's narrative. Macbeth is warned to "beware Macduff"[2] by "certeine wizzards, in whose words he put great confidence;" and the false promises were made to him by "a certeine witch, whome he had in great trust, (who) had told him that he

should neuer be slaine with man borne of anie woman, nor vanquished till the wood of Bernane came to the castell of Dunsinane."[3]

[Footnote 1: Holinshed, Scotland, p. 170, c. 2, l. 55.]

[Footnote 2: Macbeth, IV. l. 71. Holinshed, p. 174, c. 2, l. 10.]

[Footnote 3: Ibid. l. 13.]

88. In this account we find that the supernatural communications adopted by Shakspere were derived from three sources; and the contention is that he has retained two of them—the "goddesses of Destinie" and the witches; and the evidence of this retention is the third proof relied on, namely, that the stage direction in the first folio, Act IV. sc. i., is, "Enter Hecate and the *other* three witches," when three characters supposed to be witches are already upon the scene. Holinshed's narrative makes it clear that the idea of the "goddesses of Destinie" was distinctly suggested to Shakspere's mind, as well as that of the witches, as the mediums of supernatural influence. The question is, did he retain both, or did he reject one and retain the other? It can scarcely be doubted that one such influence running through the play would conduce to harmony and unity of idea; and as Shakspere, not a servile follower of his source in any case, has interwoven in "Macbeth" the totally distinct narrative of the murder of King Duffe,[1] it is hardly to be supposed that he would scruple to blend these two different sets of characters if any advantage were to be gained by so doing. As to the stage direction in the first folio, it is difficult to see what it would prove, even supposing that the folio were the most scrupulous piece of editorial work thathad ever been effected. It presupposes that the "weird sisters" are on the stage as well as the witches. But it is perfectly clear that the witches continue the dialogue; so the other more powerful beings must be supposed to be standing silent in the background—a suggestion so monstrous that it is hardly necessary to refer to the slovenliness of the folio stage directions to show how unsatisfactory an argument based upon one of them must be.

[Footnote 1: Ibid. p. 149. "A sort of witches dwelling in a towne of Murreyland called Fores" (c. 2, l. 30) were prominent in this account.]

89. The evidence of Forman and Holinshed has been stated fully, in order that the reader may be in possession of all the materials that may be necessary for forming an accurate judgment upon the point in question; but it seems to be less relied upon than the supposition that the appearance and powers of the beings in the admittedly genuine part of the third scene of the first act are not those formerly attributed to witches, and that Shakspere, having once decided to represent Norns, would never have degraded them "to three old women, who are called by Paddock and Graymalkin, sail in sieves, kill swine, serve Hecate, and deal in all the common charms, illusions, and incantations of vulgar witches. The three who 'look not like the inhabitants o' th' earth, and yet are on't;' they who can 'look into the seeds of time, and say which grain will grow;' they who seem corporal, but melt into the air, like bubbles of the earth; the weyward sisters, who make themselves air, and have in them more than mortal knowledge, are not beings of this stamp."[1]

[Footnote 1: New Shakspere Society Transactions, vol. i. p.342; Fleay's Shakspere Manual, p. 248.]

90. Now, there is a great mass of contemporary evidence to show that these supposed characteristics of the Norns are, in fact, some of the chief attributes of the witches of the sixteenth and seventeenth centuries. If this be so—if it can be proved that the supposed "goddesses of Destinie" of the play in reality possess no higher powers than could be acquired by ordinary communication with evil spirits, then no weight must be attached to the vague stage direction in the folio, occurring as it does in a volume notorious for the extreme carelessness with which it was produced; and it must be admitted that the "goddesses of Destinie"

of Holinshed were sacrificed for the sake of the witches. If, in addition to this, it can be shown that there was a very satisfactory reason why the witches should have been chosen as the representatives of the evil influence instead of the

Norns, the argument will be as complete as it is possible to make it.

91. But before proceeding to examine the contemporary evidence, it is necessary, in order to obtain a complete conception of the mythological view of the weird sisters, to notice a piece of criticism that is at once an expansion of, and a variation upon, the theory just stated.[1] It is suggested that the sisters of

"Macbeth" are but three in number, but that Shakspere drew upon Scandinavian mythology for a portion of the material he used in constructing these characters, and that he derived the rest from the traditions of contemporary witchcraft; in fact, that the "sisters" are hybrids between Norns and witches. The supposed proof of this is that each sister exercises the special function of one of the Norns.

"The third is the special prophetess, whilst the first takes cognizance of the past, and the second of the present, in affairs connected with humanity. These are the tasks of Urda, Verdandi, and Skulda. The first begins by asking, 'When shall we three meet again?' The second decides the time: 'When the battle's lost or won.'

The third, the future prophesies: 'That will be ere set of sun.' The first again asks,

'Where?' The second decides: 'Upon the heath.' The third, the future prophesies:

'There to meet with Macbeth.'" But their *rôle* is most clearly brought out in the famous "Hails":—

1st. Urda. [Past.] All hail, Macbeth! hail to thee, Thane of Glamis!

2nd. Verdandi. [Present.] All hail, Macbeth! hail to thee, Thane of Cawdor!

3rd. Skulda. All hail, Macbeth! thou shalt be king hereafter.[2]

This sequence is supposed to be retained in other of the sisters' speeches; but a perusal of these will soon show that it is only in the second of the above quotations that it is recognizable with any definiteness; and this, it must be remembered, is an almost verbal transcript from Holinshed, and not an original conception of Shakspere's, who might feel himself quite justified in changing the characters of the speakers, while retaining their utterances. In addition to this, the natural sequence is in many cases utterly and unnecessarily violated; as, for instance, in Act I. sc. iii., where Urda, who should be solely occupied with past matters, predicts, with extreme minuteness, the results that are to follow from her projected voyage to Aleppo, and that without any expression of resentment, but rather with promise of assistance, from Skulda, whose province she is thus

invading.

[Footnote 1: In a letter to *The Academy*, 8th February, 1879, signed

"Charlotte Carmichael."]

[Footnote 2: I have taken the liberty of printing this quotation as it stands in the text. The writer in *The Academy* has effected a rearrangement of the dialogue by importing what might be Macbeth's replies to the three sisters from his speech beginning at l. 70, and alternating them with the different "Hails," which, in addition, are not correctly quoted—for what purpose it is difficult to see. It may be added here that in a subsequent number of *The Academy*, a long letter upon the same subject appeared from Mr. Karl Blind, which seems to prove little except the author's erudition. He assumes the Teutonic origin of the sisters throughout, and, consequently, adduces little evidence in favour of the theory.

One of his points is the derivation of the word "weird" or

"wayward," which, as will be shown subsequently, was applied to witches. Another point is, that the witch scenes savour strongly of the staff-rime of old German poetry. It is interesting to find two upholders of the Norn-theory relying mainly for proof of their position upon a scene (Act I. sc. i.) which Mr Fleay says that the very statement of this theory (p. 249) must brand as spurious. The question of the sisters' beards too, regarding which Mr. Blind brings somewhat far-fetched evidence, is, I think, more satisfactorily settled by the quotations in the text.]

92. But this latter piece of criticism seems open to one grave objection to which the former is not liable. Mr. Fleay separates the portions of the play which are undoubtedly to be assigned to witches from the parts he gives to his Norns, and attributes them to different characters; the other mixes up the witch and Norn elements in one confused mass. The earlier critic saw the absurdity of such a supposition when he wrote: "Shakspere may have raised the wizard and witches of the latter parts of Holinshed to the weird sisters of the former parts, but the converse process is impossible."[1] Is it conceivable that Shakspere, who, as most people admit, was a man of some poetic feeling, being in possession of the beautiful Norn-legend—the silent Fate-goddesses sitting at the foot of Igdrasil, the mysterious tree of human existence, and watering its roots with water from the sacred spring—could, ruthlessly and without cause, mar the charm of the legend by the gratuitous introduction of the gross and primarily unpoetical details incident to the practice of witchcraft? No man with a glimmer of poetry in his soul will imagine it for a moment. The separation of characters is more credible than this; but if that theory can be shown to be unfounded, there is no

improbability in supposing that Shakspere, finding that the question of witchcraft was, in consequence of events that had taken place not long before the time of the production of "Macbeth," absorbing the attention of all men, from king to peasant, should set himself to deal with such a popular subject, and, by the magic of his art, so raise it out of its degradation into the region of poetry, that men should wonder and say, "Can this be witchcraft indeed?"

[Footnote 1: Shakspere Manual, p. 249.]

93. In comparing the evidence to be deduced from the contemporary records of witchcraft with the sayings and doings of the sisters in "Macbeth," those parts of the play will first be dealt with upon which no doubt as to their genuineness has ever been cast, and which are asserted to be solely applicable to Norns. If it can be shown that these describe witches rather than Norns, the position that Shakspere intentionally substituted witches for the "goddesses of Destinie"

mentioned in his authority is practically unassailable. First, then, it is asserted that the description of the appearance of the sisters given by Banquo applies to Norns rather than witches—

"They look not like the inhabitants o' th' earth, And yet are on't."

This question of applicability, however, must not be decided by the consideration of a single sentence, but of the whole passage from which it is extracted; and, whilst considering it, it should be carefully borne in mind that it occurs immediately before those lines which are chiefly relied upon as proving the identity of the sisters with Urda, Verdandi, and Skulda.

Banquo, on seeing the sisters, says—

"What are these,

So withered and so wild in their attire,

That look not like the inhabitants o' th' earth,

And yet are on't? Live you, or are you aught

That man may question? You seem to understand me, By each at once her chappy finger laying

Upon her skinny lips: you should be women,

And yet your beards forbid me to interpret

That you are so."

It is in the first moment of surprise that the sisters, appearing so suddenly, seem to Banquo unlike the inhabitants of this earth. When he recovers from the shock and is capable of deliberate criticism, he sees chappy fingers, skinny lips—in fact, nothing to distinguish them from poverty-stricken, ugly old women but their beards. A more accurate poetical counterpart to the prose descriptions given by contemporary writers of the appearance of the poor creatures who were charged with the crime of witchcraft could hardly have been penned. Scot, for instance, says, "They are women which commonly be old, lame, bleare-eied, pale, fowle, and full of wrinkles…. They are leane and deformed, showing melancholie in their faces;"[1] and Harsnet describes a witch as "an old weather-beaten crone, having her chin and knees meeting for age, walking like a bow, leaning on a staff, hollow-eyed, untoothed, furrowed, having her lips trembling with palsy, going mumbling in the streets; one that hath forgotten her Pater-noster, yet hath a shrewd tongue to call a drab a drab."[2] It must be remembered that these accounts are by two sceptics, who saw nothing in the witches but poor, degraded old women. In a description which assumes their supernatural power such minute details would not be possible; yet there is quite enough in Banquo's description to suggest neglect, squalor, and misery. But if this were not so, there is one feature in the description of the sisters that would settle the question once and for ever. The beard was in Elizabethan times the recognized characteristic of the witch. In one old play it is said, "The women that come to us for disguises must wear beards, and that's to say a token of a witch;"[3] and in another, "Some women have beards; marry, they are half witches;"[4] and Sir Hugh Evans gives decisive testimony to the fact when he says of the disguised Falstaff, "By yea and no, I think, the 'oman is a witch indeed: I like not when a 'oman has a great peard; I spy a great peard under her muffler."[5]

[Footnote 1: Discoverie, book i. ch. 3, p. 7.]

[Footnote 2: Harsnet, Declaration, p. 136.]

[Footnote 3: Honest Man's Fortune, II. i. Furness, Variorum, p. 30.]

[Footnote 4: Dekker's Honest Whore, sc. x. l. 126.]

[Footnote 5: Merry Wives of Windsor, Act IV. sc. ii.]

94. Every item of Banquo's description indicates that he is speaking of witches; nothing in it is incompatible with that supposition. Will it apply with equal force

to Norns? It can hardly be that these mysterious mythical beings, who exercise an incomprehensible yet powerful influence over human destiny, could be described with any propriety in terms so revolting. A veil of wild, weird grandeur might be thrown around them; but can it be supposed that Shakspere would degrade them by representing them with chappy fingers, skinny lips, and beards? It is particularly to be noticed, too, that although in this passage he is making an almost verbal transcript from Holinshed, these details are interpolated without the authority of the chronicle. Let it be supposed, for an instant, that the text ran thus—

Banquo. ... What are these

So withered and so wild in their attire,[1]

That look not like the inhabitants o' th' earth,

And yet are on't?[2] Live you, or are you ought

That man may question?[3]

Macbeth. Speak if you can, what are you?

90

1st Witch. All hail, Macbeth! hail to thee, thane of Glamis![4]

2nd Witch. All hail, Macbeth! hail to thee, thane of Cawdor![5]

3rd Witch. All hail, Macbeth! thou shall be king hereafter.[6]

This is so accurate a dramatization of the parallel passage in Holinshed, and so entire in itself, that there is some temptation to ask whether it was not so written at first, and the interpolated lines subsequently inserted by the author. Whether this be so or not, the question must be put—Why, in such a passage, did Shakspere insert three lines of most striking description of the appearance of witches? Can any other reason be suggested than that he had made up his mind to replace the "goddesses of Destinie" by the witches, and had determined that there should be no possibility of any doubt arising about it?

[Footnote 1: Three women in strange and wild apparel,]

[Footnote 2: resembling creatures of elder world,]

[Footnote 3: whome when they attentivelie beheld, woondering much at the sight, the first of them spake and said;]

[Footnote 4: 'All haile, Makbeth, thane of Glammis' (for he had latelie entered into that dignitie and office by the death of his father Sinell).]

[Footnote 5: The second of them said; 'Haile, Makbeth, thane of Cawder.']

[Footnote 6: But the third said; 'All haile, Makbeth, that heereafter shalt be king of Scotland.']

95. The next objection is, that the sisters exercise powers that witches did not possess. They can "look into the seeds of time, and say which grain will grow, and which will not." In other words, they foretell

future events, which witches could not do. But this is not the fact. The recorded witch trials teem with charges of having prophesied what things were about to happen; no charge is more common. The following, quoted by Charles Knight in his biography of Shakspere, might almost have suggested the simile in the last-mentioned lines.

Johnnet Wischert is "indicted for passing to the green growing corn in May, twenty-two years since or thereby, sitting thereupon tymous in the morning before the sun-rising, and being there found and demanded what she was doing, thou[1] answered, I shall tell thee; I have been peeling the blades of the corn. I find it will be a dear year, the blade of the corn grows withersones [contrary to the course of the sun], and when it grows sonegatis about [with the course of the sun] it will be good cheap year."[2] The following is another apt illustration of the power, which has been translated from the unwieldy Lowland Scotch account of the trial of Bessie Roy in 1590. The Dittay charged her thus: "You are indicted and accused that whereas, when you were dwelling with William King in Barra, about twelve years ago, or thereabouts, and having gone into the field to pluck lint with other women, in their presence made a compass in the earth, and a hole in the midst thereof; and afterwards, by thy conjurations thou causedst a great worm to come up first out of the said hole, and creep over the compass; and next a little worm came forth, which crept over also; and last [thou] causedst a great worm to come forth, which could not pass over the compass, but fell down and died. Which enchantment and witchcraft thou interpretedst in this form: that the first great worm that crept over the compass was the goodman William King, who should live; and the little worm was a child in the goodwife's womb, who was unknown to any one to be with child, and that the child should live; and, thirdly, the last great worm thou interpretedst to be the goodwife, who should die: *which came to pass after thy speaking*."[3] Surely there could hardly be plainer instances of looking "into the seeds of time, and saying which grain will

grow, and which will not," than these.

[Footnote 1: Sic.]

[Footnote 2: p. 438.]

[Footnote 3: Pitcairn, I. ii. 207. Cf. also Ibid. pp. 212, 213, and 231, where the crime is described as "foreknowledge."]

96. Perhaps this is the most convenient place for pointing out the full meaning of the first scene of "Macbeth," and its necessary connection with the rest of the play. It is, in fact, the fag-end of a witches' sabbath, which, if fully represented, would bear a strong resemblance to the scene at the commencement of the fourth act. But a long scene on such a subject would be tedious and unmeaning at the commencement of the play. The audience is therefore left to assume that the witches have met, performed their conjurations, obtained from the evil spirits the information concerning Macbeth's career that they desired to obtain, and perhaps have been commanded by the fiends to perform the mission they subsequently carry through. All that is needed for the dramatic effect is a slight hint of probable diabolical interference, and that Macbeth is to be the special object of it; and this is done in as artistic a manner as is perhaps imaginable. In the first scene they obtain their information; in the second they utter their prediction.

Every minute detail of these scenes is based upon the broad, recognized facts of witchcraft.

97. It is also suggested that the power of vanishing from the sight possessed by the sisters—the power to make themselves air—was not characteristic of witches. But this is another assertion that would not have been made, had the authorities upon the subject been investigated with only slight attention. No feature of the crime of witchcraft is better attested than this; and the modern witch of story-books is still represented as riding on a broomstick—a relic of the enchanted rod with which the devil used to provide his worshippers, upon which to come to his sabbaths.[1] One of the charges in the indictment against the notorious Dr. Fian ran thus: "Fylit for suffering himself to be careit to North Berwik kirk, as if he had bene souchand athoirt [whizzing above] the eird."[2]

Most effectual ointments were prepared for effecting this method of locomotion, which have been recorded, and are given below[3] as an illustration of the wild kind of recipes which Shakspere rendered more grim in his caldron scene. The efficacy of these ointments is well illustrated by a story narrated by Reginald

Scot, which unfortunately, on account of certain incidents, cannot be given in his own terse words. The hero of it happened to be staying temporarily with a friend, and on one occasion found her rubbing her limbs with a certain preparation, and mumbling the while. After a time she vanished out of his sight; and he, being curious to investigate the affair, rubbed himself with the remaining ointment, and almost immediately he found himself transported a long distance through the air, and deposited right in the very midst of a witches' sabbath. Naturally alarmed, he cried out, "'In the name of God, what make I heere?' and upon those words the whole assemblie vanished awaie."[4]

[Footnote 1: Scot, book iii. ch. iii. p. 43.]

[Footnote 2: Pitcairn, I. ii. 210. Cf. also Ibid. p. 211. Scot, book iii. ch. vii. p.

51.]

[Footnote 3: "Sundrie receipts and ointments made and used for the transportation of witches, and other miraculous effects.

"Rx. The fat of yoong children, & seeth it with water in a brazen vessell, reseruing the thickest of that which remaineth boiled in the bottome, which they laie up & keep untill occasion serveth to use it. They put hereinto Eleoselinum, Aconitum, frondes populeas, & Soote." This is given almost verbatim in Middleton's Witch.

"Rx. Sium, Acarum Vulgare, Pentaphyllon, the bloud of a Flittermouse, Solanum Somniferum, & oleum."

It would seem that fern seed had the same virtue.—I Hen. IV. II. i.]

[Footnote 4: Scot, book iii. ch. vi. p. 46.]

98. The only vestige of a difficulty, therefore, that remains is the use of the term"weird sisters" in describing the witches. It is perfectly clear that Holinshed used these words as a sort of synonym for the "goddesses of Destinie;" but with such a mass of evidence as has been produced to show that Shakspere elected to introduce witches in the place of the Norns, it surely would not be unwarrantable to suppose that he might retain this term as a poetical and not unsuitable description of the characters to whom it was applied. And this is the less improbable as it can be shown that both words were at times applied to witches.

As the quotation given subsequently[1] proves, the Scotch witches were in the

habit of speaking of the frequenters of a particular sabbath as "the sisters;" and in Heywood's "Witches of Lancashire," one of the characters says about a certain act of supposed witchcraft, "I remember that some three months since I crossed a wayward woman; one that I now suspect."[2]

[Footnote 1: § 107, p. 114.]

[Footnote 2: Act V. sc. iii.]

99. Here, then, in the very stronghold of the supposed proof of the Norn-theory, it is possible to extract convincing evidence that the sisters are intended to be merely witches. It is not surprising that other portions of the play in which the sisters are mentioned should confirm this view. Banquo, upon hearing the fulfilment of the prophecy of the second witch, clearly expresses his opinion of the origin of the "foreknowledge" he has received, in the exclamation, "What, can the devil speak true?" For the devil most emphatically spoke through the witches; but how could he in

any sense be said to speak through Norns? Again, Macbeth informs his wife that on his arrival at Forres, he made inquiry into the amount of reliance that could be placed in the utterances of the witches, "and learned by the perfectest report that they had more in them than mortal knowledge."[1] This would be possible enough if witches were the subjects of the investigation, for their chief title to authority would rest upon the general opinion current in the neighbourhood in which they dwelt; but how could such an inquiry be carried out successfully in the case of Norns? It is noticeable, too, that Macbeth knows exactly where to find the sisters when he wants them; and when he says—

"More shall they speak; for now I am bent to know, By the worst means, the worst,"[2]he makes another clear allusion to the traffic of the witches with the devil. After the events recorded in Act IV. sc. i., Macbeth speaks of the prophecies upon which he relies as "the equivocation of the fiend,"[3] and the prophets as "these juggling fiends;"[4] and with reason —for he has seen and heard the very devils themselves, the masters of the witches and sources of all their evil power. Every point in the play that bears upon the subject at all tends to show that Shakspere intentionally replaced the "goddesses of Destinie" by witches; and that the supposed Norn origin of these characters is the result of a somewhat too great eagerness to unfold a novel and startling theory.

[Footnote 1: Act I. sc. v. l. 2.]

[Footnote 2: Mr. Fleay avoids the difficulty created by this passage, which alludes to the witches as "the weird sisters," by supposing that these lines were interpolated by Middleton—a method of criticism that hardly needs comment.

Act III. sc. iv. l. 134.]

[Footnote 3: Act V. sc. v. l. 43.]

[Footnote 4: Ibid. sc. viii. l. 19.]

100. Assuming, therefore, that the witch-nature of the sisters is conclusively proved, it now becomes necessary to support the assertion previously made, that good reason can be shown why Shakspere should have elected to represent witches rather than Norns.

It is impossible to read "Macbeth" without noticing the prominence given to the belief that witches had the power of creating storms and other atmospheric disturbances, and that they delighted in so doing. The sisters elect to meet in thunder, lightning, or rain. To them "fair is foul, and foul is fair," as they "hover through the fog and filthy air." The whole of the earlier part of the third scene of the first act is one blast of tempest with its attendant devastation. They can loose and bind the winds,[1] cause vessels to be tempest-tossed at sea, and mutilate wrecked bodies.[2] They describe themselves as "posters of the sea and land;"[3]

the heath they meet upon is blasted;[4] and they vanish "as breath into the wind."

[5] Macbeth conjures them to answer his questions thus:—

"Though you untie the winds, and let them fight Against the churches; though the yesty waves

Confound and swallow navigation up;

Though bladed corn be lodged, and trees blown down; Though castles topple on their warders' heads;

Though palaces and pyramids do slope

Their heads to their foundations; though the treasure Of nature's germens tumble all together,

Even till destruction sicken."[6]

[Footnote 1: I. iii. 11, 12.]

[Footnote 2: Act I. sc. iii. l. 28.]

[Footnote 3: Ibid. l. 32.]

[Footnote 4: Ibid. l. 77.]

[Footnote 5: Ibid. ll. 81, 82.]

[Footnote 6: Act IV. sc. i. ll. 52-60.]

101. Now, this command over the elements does not form at all a prominent feature in the English records of witchcraft. A few isolated charges of the kind may be found. In 1565, for instance, a witch was burnt who confessed that she had caused all the tempests that had taken place in that year. Scot, too, has a few short sentences upon this subject, but does not give it the slightest prominence.

[1] Nor in the earlier Scotch trials recorded by Pitcairn does this charge appear amongst the accusations against the witches. It is exceedingly curious to notice the utter harmless nature of the charges brought against the earlier culprits; and how, as time went on and the panic increased, they gradually deepened in colour, until no act was too gross, too repulsive, or too ridiculously impossible to be excluded from the indictment. The following quotations from one of the earliest reported trials are given because they illustrate most forcibly the condition of the poor women who were supposed to be witches, and the real basis of fact upon which the belief in the crime subsequently built itself.

[Footnote 1: Book iii. ch. 13, p. 60.]

102. Bessie Dunlop was tried for witchcraft in 1576. One of the principal accusations against her was that she held intercourse with a devil who appeared to her in the shape of a neighbour of hers, one Thom Reed, who had recently died. Being asked how and where she met Thom

Reed, she said, "As she was gangand betwixt her own house and the yard of Monkcastell, dryvand her ky to the pasture, and makand heavy sair dule with herself, gretand[1] very fast for her cow that was dead, her husband and child that wer lyand sick in the land ill, and she new risen out of gissane,[2] the aforesaid Thom met her by the way, healsit[3] her, and said, 'Gude day, Bessie,' and she said, 'God speed you, guidman.' 'Sancta Marie,' said he, 'Bessie, why makes thow sa great dule and sair greting for ony wardlie thing?' She answered 'Alas! have I not great cause to make great dule, for our gear is trakit,[4] and my husband is on the point of deid, and one babie of my own will not live, and myself at ane weak point; have I not gude cause then to have ane sair hart?' But Thom said, 'Bessie, thou hastcrabit[5] God, and askit some thing you suld not have done; and tharefore I counsell thee to mend to Him, for I tell thee thy barne sall die and the seik cow, or you come hame; and thy twa sheep shall die too; but thy husband shall mend, and shall be as hale and fair as ever he was.' And then I was something blyther, for he tauld me that my guidman would mend. Then Thom Reed went away fra me in through the yard of Monkcastell, and I thought that he gait in at ane narrower hole of the dyke nor anie erdlie man culd have gone throw, and swa I was something fleit."[6]

[Footnote 1: Weeping. I have only half translated this passage, for I feared to spoil the sad simplicity of it.]

[Footnote 2: Child-bed.]

[Footnote 3: Saluted.]

[Footnote 4: Dwindled away.]

[Footnote 5: Displeased.]

[Footnote 6: Frightened.]

This was the first time that Thom appeared to her. On the third occasion he asked her "if she would not trow[1] in him." She said "she would trow in ony bodye did her gude." Then Thom promised her much wealth if she would deny her christendom. She answered that "if she should be riven at horsis taillis, she suld never do that, but promised to be leal and trew to him in ony thing she could do,"

whereat he was angry.

[Footnote 1: Trust.]

On the fourth occasion, the poor woman fell further into sin, and accompanied Thom to a fairy meeting. Thom asked her to join the party; but she said "she saw na proffeit to gang thai kind of gaittis, unless she kend wherefor." Thom offered the old inducement, wealth; but she replied that "she dwelt with her awin husband and bairnis," and could not leave them. And so Thom began to be very crabit with her, and said, "if so she thought, she would get lytill gude of him."

She was then demanded if she had ever asked any favour of Thom for herself or any other person. She answered that "when sundrie persons came to her to seek

help for their beast, their cow, or ewe, or for any barne that was tane away with ane evill blast of wind, or elf grippit, she gait and speirit[1] at Thom what myght help them; and Thom would pull ane herb and gif her out of his awin hand, and bade her scheir[2] the same with ony other kind of herbis, and oppin the beistes mouth, and put thame in, and the beist wald mend."[3]

[Footnote 1: Inquired.]

[Footnote 2: Chop.]

[Footnote 3: Pitcairn, I. ii. 51, et seq.]

It seems hardly possible to believe that a story like this, which is half marred by the attempt to partially modernize its simple pathetic language, and which would probably bring a tear to the eye, if not a shilling from the pocket, of the most unsympathetic being of the present day, should be considered sufficient three hundred years ago, to convict the narrator of a crime worthy of death; yet so it was. This sad picture of the breakdown of a poor woman's intellect in the unequal struggle against poverty and sickness is only made visible to us by the light of the flames that, mercifully to her perhaps, took poor Bessie Dunlop away for ever from the sick husband, and weakly children, and the "ky," and the humble hovel where they all dwelt together, and from the daily, heart-rending, almost hopeless struggle to obtain enough food to keep life in the bodies of this miserable family. The historian—who makes it his chief anxiety to record, to the minutest and most irrelevant details, the deeds, noble or ignoble, of those who have managed to stamp their names upon the muster-roll of Fame—turns carelessly or scornfully the page which contains such insignificant matter as this; but those who believe

"That not a worm is cloven in vain;

That not a moth with vain desire

Is shrivel'd in a fruitless fire,

Or but subserves another's gain," will hardly feel that poor Bessie's life and death were entirely without their meaning.

103. As the trials for witchcraft increase, however, the details grow more and more revolting; and in the year 1590 we find a most extraordinary batch of cases

—extraordinary for the monstrosity of the charges contained in them, and alsofor the fact that this feature, so insisted upon in Macbeth, the raising of winds and storms, stands out in extremely bold relief. The explanation of this is as follows. In the year 1589, King James VI. brought his bride, Anne of Denmark, home to Scotland. During the voyage an unusually violent storm raged, which scattered the vessels composing the royal escort, and, it would appear, caused the destruction of one of them. By a marvellous chance, the king's ship was driven by a wind which blew directly contrary to that which filled the sails of the other vessels;[1] and the king and queen were both placed in extreme jeopardy. James, who seems to have been as perfectly convinced of the reality of witchcraft as he was of his own infallibility, at once came to the conclusion that the storm had been raised by the aid of evil spirits, for the express purpose of getting rid of so powerful an enemy of the Prince of Darkness as the righteous king. The result was that a rigorous investigation was made into the whole affair; a great number of persons were tried for attempting the king's life by witchcraft; and that prince, undeterred by the apparent impropriety of being judge in what was, in reality, his own cause, presided at many of the trials, condescended to superintend the tortures applied to the accused in order to extort a confession, and even went so far in one case as to write a letter to the judges commanding a condemnation.

[Footnote 1: Pitcairn, I. ii. 218.]

104. Under these circumstances, considering who the prosecutor was, and who the judge, and the effectual methods at the service of the court for extorting confessions,[1] it is not surprising that the king's surmises were fully justified by the statements of the accused. It is impossible to read these without having parts of the witch-scenes in "Macbeth" ringing in the ears like an echo. John Fian, a young schoolmaster, and leader of the gang, or "coven" as it was called, was charged with having caused the leak in the king's ship, and with having raised the wind and created a mist for the purpose of hindering his voyage.[2] On another occasion he and several other witches entered into a ship, and caused it to perish.[3] He was also able by witchcraft to open locks.[4] He visited churchyards at night, and dismembered bodies for his charms; the bodies of unbaptized infants being preferred.[5]

[Footnote 1: The account of the tortures inflicted upon Fian are too horrible for quotation.]

[Footnote 2: Pitcairn, I. ii. 211.]

[Footnote 3: Ibid. 212. He confessed that Satan commanded him to chase cats"purposlie to be cassin into the sea to raise windis for destructioune of schippis."

Macbeth, I. iii. 15-25.]

[Footnote 4: "Fylit for opening of ane loke be his sorcerie in David Seytounis moderis, be blawing in ane woman's hand, himself sittand att the fyresyde."—

See also the case of Bessie Roy, I. ii. 208. The English method of opening locks was more complicated than the Scotch, as will appear from the following quotation from Scot, book xii. ch. xiv. p. 246:—

"A charme to open locks. Take a peece of wax crossed in baptisme, and doo but print certeine floures therein, and tie them in the hinder skirt of your shirt; and when you would undoo the locke, blow thrice therein, saieing, 'Arato hoc partico hoc maratarykin; I open this doore in thy name that I am forced to breake, as thou brakest hell gates. In nomine patris etc. Amen.'" Macbeth, IV. i. 46.]

[Footnote 5:

"Finger of birth-strangled babe,

Ditch-delivered by a drab."

Macbeth, IV. i. 30.]

Agnes Sampsoune confessed to the king that to compass his death she took a black toad and hung it by the hind legs for three days, and collected the venom that fell from it. She said that if she could have obtained a piece of linen that the king had worn, she could have destroyed his life with this venom; "causing him such extraordinarie paines as if he had beene lying upon sharpe thornes or endis of needles."[1] She went out to sea to a vessel called *The Grace of God*, and

when she came away the devil raised a wind, and the vessel was wrecked.
[2] She delivered a letter from Fian to another witch, which was to this
effect: "Ye sall warne the rest of the sisteris to raise the winde this day at
ellewin houris to stay the queenis cuming in Scotland."[3]

[Footnote 1: Pitcairn, I. ii. 218.

"Toad, that under cold stone

Days and nights has thirty-one

Sweltered venom sleeping got."

Macbeth, IV. i. 6.]

[Footnote 2: Ibid. 235.]

[Footnote 3: Ibid. 236.]

This is her confession as to the methods adopted for raising the
storm. "At the time when his Majestie was in Denmarke, shee being
accompanied by the parties before speciallie named, took a cat and
christened it, and afterwards bounde to each part of that cat the cheefest
parts of a dead man, and the severall joyntes of his bodie; and that in the
night following the said cat was conveyed into the middest of the sea by
all these witches, sayling in their riddles or cives,[1] as is afore said, and
so left the said cat right before the town of Leith in Scotland. This done,
there did arise such a tempest in the sea as a greater hath not been seene,
which tempest was the cause of the perishing of a vessell coming over
from the town of Brunt Ilande to the town of Leith.... Againe, it is
confessed that the said christened cat was the cause that the kinges
Majesties shippe at his coming forth of Denmarke had a contrarie wind to
the rest of his shippes...."[2]

[Footnote 1: Macbeth, I. iii. 8.]

104

[Footnote 2: Pitcairn, Reprint of Newes from Scotland, I. ii. 218. See also Trial of Ewsame McCalgane, I. ii. 254.]

105. It is worth a note that this art of going to sea in sieves, which Shakspere has referred to in his drama, seems to have been peculiar to this set of witches.

English witches had the reputation of being able to go upon the water in egg-shells and cockle-shells, but seem never to have detected any peculiar advantages in the sieve. Not so these Scotch witches. Agnes told the king that she, "with a great many other witches, to the number of two hundreth, all together went to sea, each one in a riddle or cive, and went into the same very substantially, with flaggons of wine, making merrie, and drinking by the way in the same riddles or cives, to the kirke of North Barrick in Lowthian, and that after they landed they tooke hands on the lande and daunced a reill or short daunce." They then opened the graves and took the fingers, toes, and knees of the bodies to make charms.[1]

[Footnote 1: Pitcairn, I. ii. 217.]

It can be easily understood that these trials created an intense excitement in

Scotland. The result was that a tract was printed, containing a full account of all the principal incidents; and the fact that this pamphlet was reprinted once, if not twice,[1] in London, shows that interest in the affair spread south of the Border; and this is confirmed by the publisher's prefatorial apology, in which he states that the pamphlet was printed to prevent the public from being imposed upon by unauthorized and extravagant statements of what had taken place.[2] Under ordinary circumstances, events of this nature would form a nine days' wonder, and then die a natural death; but in this particular case the public interest continued for an abnormal time; for eight years subsequent to the date of the trials, James published his "Daemonologie"—a work founded to a great extent upon his experiences at the trials of 1590. This was a sign to both England and Scotland that the subject of witchcraft was still of engrossing interest to him; and as he was then the fully recognized heir-apparent to the English crown, the publication of such a work would not fail to induce a great amount of attention to the subject dealt with. In 1603 he ascended the English throne. His first parliament met on the 19th of March, 1604, and on the 27th of the same month a bill was brought into the House of Lords dealing with the question of witchcraft.

It was referred to a committee of which twelve bishops were members; and this committee, after much debating, came to the conclusion that the bill was imperfect. In consequence of this a fresh one was drawn, and by the 9th of June a statute had passed both Houses of Parliament, which enacted, among other things, that "if any person shall practise or exercise any invocation or conjuration of any evil or wicked spirit, or shall consult with, entertain, feed, or reward any evil and wicked spirit,[3] or take up any dead man, woman, or child out of his, her, or their grave ... or the skin, bone, or any other part of any dead person to be employed or used in any manner of witchcraft,[4] ... or shall ... practise ... any witchcraft ... whereby any person shall be killed, wasted, pined, or lamed in his or her body or any part thereof,[5] such offender shall suffer the pains of death as felons, without benefit of clergy or sanctuary." Hutchinson, in his "Essay on Witchcraft," published in 1720, declares that this statute was framed expressly to meet the offences exposed by the trials of 1590-1; but, although this cannot be conclusively proved, yet it is not at all improbable that the hurry with which the statute was passed into law immediately upon the accession of James, would recall to the public mind the interest he had taken in those trials in particular and the subject in general, and that Shakspere producing, as nearly all the critics agree, his tragedy at about this date, should draw upon his memory for the half-forgotten details of those trials, and thus embody in "Macbeth" the allusions to them that have been pointed out— much less accurately than he did in the case of the Babington affair, because the facts had been far less carefully recorded, and

the time at which his attention had been called to them far more remote.[6]

[Footnote 1: One copy of this reprint bears the name of W. Wright, another that of Thomas Nelson. The full title is—

"Newes from Scotland,

"Declaring the damnable life of Doctor Fian, a notable Sorcerer, who was burned at Edenborough in Januarie last, 1591; which Doctor was Register to the Deuill, that sundrie times preached at North Barricke kirke to a number of notorious witches; with the true examinations of the said Doctor and witches as they uttered them in the presence of the Scottish king: Discouering how they pretended to bewitch and drowne his Majestie in the sea, comming from Denmarke, with such other wonderfull matters, as the like hath not bin heard at anie time.

"Published according to the Scottish copie.

"Printed for William Wright."]

[Footnote 2: These events are referred to in an existing letter by the notorious Thos. Phelippes to Thos. Barnes, Cal. State Papers (May 21, 1591), 1591-4, p.

38.]

[Footnote 3: Such as Paddock, Graymalkin, and Harpier.]

[Footnote 4: "Liver of blaspheming Jew," etc.—Macbeth, IV. i. 26.]

[Footnote 5:

"I will drain him dry as hay;

Sleep shall neither night nor day

Hang upon his pent-house lid;

He shall live a man forbid:

Weary se'nnights, nine times nine,

Shall he dwindle, peak, and pine."

Macbeth, I. iii. 18-23.]

[Footnote 6: The excitement about the details of the witch trials would culminate

in 1592. Harsnet's book would be read by Shakspere in 1603.]

106. There is one other mode of temptation which was adopted by the evil spirits, implicated to a great extent with the traditions of witchcraft, but nevertheless more suitably handled as a separate subject, which is of so gross and revolting a nature that it should willingly be passed over in silence, were it not for the fact that the belief in it was, as Scot says, "so stronglie and universallie received" in the times of Elizabeth and James.

From the very earliest period of the Christian era the affection of one sex for the other was considered to be under the special control of the devil. Marriage was to be tolerated; but celibacy was the state most conducive to the near intercourse with heaven that was so dearly sought after. This opinion was doubtless generated by the tendency of the early Christian leaders to hold up the events of the life rather than the teachings of the sacred Founder of the sect as the one rule of conduct to be received by His followers. To have been the recipients of the stigmata was a far greater evidence of holiness and favour with Heaven than the quiet and unnoted daily practice of those virtues upon which Christ pronounced His blessing; and in less improbable matters they did not scruple, in their enthusiasm, to attempt to establish a rule of life in direct contradiction to the laws of that universe of which they professed to believe Him to be the Creator.

The futile attempt to imitate His immaculate purity blinded their eyes to the fact that He never taught or encouraged celibacy among His followers, and this gradually led them to the strange conclusion that the passion which, sublimed and brought under control, is the source of man's noblest and holiest feelings, was a prompting proceeding from the author of all evil. Imbued with this idea, religious enthusiasts of both sexes immured themselves in convents; took oaths of perpetual celibacy; and even, in certain isolated cases, sought to compromise with Heaven, and baffle the tempter, by rendering a fall impossible—forgetting that the victory over sin does not consist in immunity from temptation, but, being tempted, not to fall. But no convent walls are so strong as to shut great nature out; and even within these sacred precincts the ascetics found that they were not free from the temptations of their arch-enemy. In consequence of this, a belief sprang up, and spread from its original source into the outer world, in a class of devils called incubi and succubi, who roamed the earth with no other object than to tempt people to abandon their purity of life. The cases of assault by incubi were much more frequent than those by succubi, just as women were much more affected by the dancing manias in the fifteenth century than men;[1]

—the reason, perhaps, being that they are much less capable of resisting physicalprivation;—but, according to the belief of the Middle Ages, there was no generic difference between the incubus and succubus. Here was a belief that, when the witch fury sprang up, attached itself as a matter of course as the phase of the crime; and it was an almost universal charge against the accused that they offended in this manner with their familiars, and hundreds of poor creatures suffered death upon such an indictment. More details will be found in the authorities upon this unpleasant subject. [2]

[Footnote 1: Hecker, Epidemics of the Middle Ages, p. 136.]

[Footnote 2: Hutchinson, p. 52. The Witch of Edmonton, Act V. Scot, Discoverie, book iv.]

107. This intercourse did not, as a rule, result in offspring; but this

was not universally the case. All badly deformed or monstrous children were suspected of having had such an undesirable parentage, and there was a great tendency to believe that they ought to be destroyed. Luther was a decided advocate of this course, deeming the destruction of a life far preferable to the chance of having a devil in the family. In Drayton's poem, "The Mooncalf," one of the gossips present at the birth of the calf suggests that it ought to be buried alive as a monster.[1] Caliban is a mooncalf,[2] and his origin is distinctly traced to a source of this description. It is perfectly clear what was the one thing that the foul witch Sycorax did which prevented her life from being taken; and it would appear from this that the inhabitants of Argier were far more merciful in this respect than their European neighbours. Such a charge would have sent any woman to the stake in Scotland, without the slightest hope of mercy, and the usual plea for respite would only have been an additional reason for hastening the execution of the sentence.[3]

[Footnote 1: Ed. 1748, p. 171.]

[Footnote 2: Tempest, II. ii. 111, 115.]

[Footnote 3: Cf. Othello, I. i. 91. Titus Andronicus, IV. ii.]

108. In the preceding pages an endeavour has been made to delineate the most prominent features of a belief which the great Reformation was destined first to foster into unnatural proportions and vitality, and in the end to destroy. Up to the period of the Reformation, the creed of the nation had been practically uniform, and one set of dogmas was unhesitatingly accepted by the people as infallible,

and therefore hardly demanding critical consideration. The great upheaval of the sixteenth century rent this quiescent uniformity into shreds; doctrines until then considered as indisputable were brought within the pale of discussion, and hence there was a great diversity of opinion, not only between the supporters of the old and of the new faith, but between the Reformers themselves. This was conspicuously the case with regard to the belief in the devils and their works.

The more timid of the Reformers clung in a great measure to the Catholic opinions; a small band, under the influence possibly of that knight-errant of freedom of thought, Giordano Bruno, who exercised some considerable influence during his visit to England by means of his Oxford lectures and disputations, entirely denied the existence of evil spirits; but the great majority gave in their adherence to a creed that was the mean between the doctrines of the old faith and the new scepticism. Their strong common sense compelled them to reject the puerilities advanced as serious evidence by the Catholic Church; but they cast aside with equal vehemence and more horror the doctrines of the Bruno school. "That there are devils," says Bullinger, reduced apparently from argument to invective, "the Sadducees in times past denied, and at this day also some scarce religious, nay, rather Epicures, deny the same; who, unless they repent, shall one day feel, to their exceeding great pain and smart, both that there are devils, and that they are the tormentors and executioners of all wicked men and Epicures."[1]

[Footnote 1: Bullinger, Fourth Decade, 9th Sermon, p. 348, Parker Society.]

109. It must be remembered, too, that the emancipation from medievalism was a very gradual process, not, as we are too prone to think it, a revolution suddenly and completely effected. It was an evolution, not an explosion. There is found, in consequence, a great divergence of opinion, not only between the earliest and the later Reformers, but between the statements of the same man at different periods of his career. Tyndale, for instance, seems to have believed in the actual possession of the human body by devils;[1] and this appears to have been the opinion of the majority at the beginning of the Reformation, for the first Prayer-book of Edward VI. contained the Catholic form of exorcism for driving devils out of children, which was expunged upon revision, the doctrine of obsession having in the mean time triumphed over the older belief. It is necessary to bear these facts in mind whilst considering any attempt to depict the general bearings of a belief such as that in evil spirits; for many irreconcilable statements are to be found among the authorities; and it is the duty of the writer to sift out and

describe those views which predominated, and these must not be supposed to be proved inaccurate because a chance quotation can be produced in contradiction.

[Footnote 1: I Tyndale, p. 82. Parker Society.]

110. There is great danger, in the attempt to bring under analysis any phase of religious belief, that the method of treatment may appear unsympathetic if not irreverent. The greatest effort has been made in these pages to avoid this fault as far as possible; for, without doubt, any form of religious dogma, however barbarous, however seemingly ridiculous, if it has once been sincerely believed and trusted by any portion of mankind, is entitled to reverent treatment. No body of great and good men can at any time credit and take comfort from a lie pure and simple; and if an extinct creed appears to lack that foundation of truth which makes creeds tolerable, it is safer to assume that it had a meaning and a truthfulness, to those who held it, that lapse of time has tended to destroy, together with the creed itself, than to condemn men wholesale as knaves and hypocrites. But the particular subject which has here been dealt with will surely be considered to be specially entitled to respect, when it is remembered that it was once an integral portion of the belief of most of our best and bravest ancestors—of men and women who dared to witness to their own sincerity amidst the fires of persecution and in the solitude of exile. It has nearly all disappeared now. The terrific hierarchy of fiends, which was so real, so full of horror three hundred years ago[1], has gradually vanished away before the advent of fuller knowledge and purer faith, and is now hardly thought of, unless as a dead mediaeval myth. But let us deal tenderly with it, remembering that the day may come when the beliefs that are nearest to our hearts may be treated as open to contempt or ridicule, and the dogmas to which we most passionately cling will, "like an insubstantial pageant faded, leave not a wrack behind."

[Footnote 1: Perhaps the following prayer, contained in Thomas Becon's

"Pomander," shows more clearly than the comments of any critic the reality of the terror:—

"An infinite number of wicked angels there are, O Lord Christ, which without ceasing seek my destruction. Against this exceeding great multitude of evil spirits send Thou me Thy blessed and heavenly angels, which may deliver me from then tyranny. Thou, O Lord, hast devoured hell, and overcome the prince of darkness and all his ministers; yea, and that not for Thyself, but for those that believe in Thee. Suffer me not, therefore, to be overcome of Satan and of his

servants, but rather let me triumph over them, that I, through strong faith and help of the blessed angels, having the victory of the hellish army, may with a joyful heart say, Death, where is thy sting? Hell, where is thy victory?—and so for ever and ever magnify Thy Holy Name. Amen." Parker Society, p. 84.]

* * * * *

111. Little attempt has hitherto been made, in the way of direct proof, to show that fairies are really only a class of devils who exercise their powers in a manner less terrible and revolting than that depicted by theologians; and for this reason chiefly—that the proposition is already more than half established when it has been shown that the attributes and functions possessed by both fairy and devil are similar in kind, although differing in degree. This has already been done to a great extent in the preceding pages, where the various actions of Puck and Ariel have been shown to differ in no essential respect from those of the devils of the time; but before commencing to study this phase of supernaturalism in Shakspere's works as a whole, and as indicative, to a certain extent, of the development of his thought upon the relation of man to the invisible world about and above him, it is necessary that this identity should be admitted without a shadow of a doubt.

112. It has been shown that fairies were probably the descendants of the lesser local deities, as devils were of the more important of the

heathen gods that were overturned by the advancing wave of Christianity, although in the course of time this distinction was entirely obliterated and forgotten. It has also been shown, as before mentioned, that many of the powers exercised by fairies were in their essence similar to those exercised by devils, especially that of appearing in divers shapes. These parallels could be carried out to an almost unlimited extent; but a few proofs only need be cited to show this identity. In the mediaeval romance of "King Orfeo" fairyland has been substituted for the classical Hades.

[1] King James, in his "Daemonologie," adopts a fourfold classification of devils, one of which he names "Phairie," and co-ordinates with the incubus.[2]

The name of the devil supposed to preside at the witches' sabbaths is sometimes given as Hecat, Diana, Sybilla; sometimes Queen of Elfame,[3] or Fairie.[4]

Indeed, Shakspere's line in "The Comedy of Errors," had it not been unnecessarily tampered with by the critics—

"A fiend, a fairy, pitiless and rough,"[5]

would have conclusively proved this identity of character.

[Footnote 1: Fairy Mythology of Shakspere, Hazlitt, p. 83.]

[Footnote 2: Daemonologie, p. 69. An instance of a fairy incubus is given in the

"Life of Robin Goodfellow," Hazlitt's Fairy Mythology, p. 176.]

[Footnote 3: Pitcairn, iii. p. 162.]

[Footnote 4: Ibid. i. p. 162, and many other places.]

[Footnote 5: Fairy has been altered to "fury," but compare Peele,

Battle of Alcazar: "Fiends, fairies, hags that fight in beds of steel."]

113. The real distinction between these two classes of spirits depends on the condition of national thought upon the subject of supernaturalism in its largest sense. A belief which has little or no foundation upon indisputable phenomena must be continually passing through varying phases, and these phases will be regulated by the nature of the subjects upon which the attention of the mass of the people is most firmly concentrated. Hence, when a nation has but one religious creed, and one that has for centuries been accepted by them, almost without question or doubt, faith becomes stereotyped, and the mind assumes an attitude of passive receptivity, undisturbed by doubts or questionings. Under such conditions, a belief in evil spirits ever ready and watching to tempt a man into heresy of belief or sinful act, and thus to destroy both body and soul, although it may exist as a theoretic portion of the accepted creed, cannot possibly become a vital doctrine to be believed by the general public. It may exist as a subject for learned dispute to while away the leisure hours of divines, but cannot by any possibility obtain an influence over the thoughts and lives of their charges. Mental disturbance on questions of doctrinal importance being, for these reasons, out of the question, the attention of the people is almost entirely riveted upon questions of material ease and advantage. The little lets and hindrances of every-day life in agricultural and domestic matters are the tribulations that appeal most incessantly to the ineradicable sense of an invisible power adverse to the interests of mankind, and consequently the class of evil spirits believed in at such a time will be fairies rather than devils—malicious little spirits, who blight the growing corn; stop the butter from forming in the churn; pinch the sluttish housemaid black and blue; and whose worst act is the exchange of the baby from its cot for a fairy changeling;—beings of a naturemost exasperating to thrifty housewife and hard-handed farmer, but nevertheless not irrevocably prejudiced against humanity, and easily to be pacified and reduced into a state of fawning friendship by such little attentions as could be rendered without difficulty by the poorest cotter. The whole fairy mythology is perfumed with an honest, healthy, careless joy in life, and a freedom from mental doubt. "I love true lovers, honest men, good fellowes, good huswives, good meate, good drinke, and all things that good is, but nothing that is

ill," declares Robin Goodfellow;[1] and this jovial materialism only reflects the state of mind of the folk who were not unwilling to believe that this lively little spirit might be seen of nights busying himself in their houses by the dying embers of the deserted fire.

[Footnote 1: Hazlitt, Fairy Mythology, p. 182.]

114. Such seems to have been the condition of England immediately before the period of the great Reformation. But with the progress of that revolution of thought the condition changes. The one true and eternal creed, as it had been deemed, is shattered for ever. Men who have hitherto accepted their religious convictions in much the same way as they had succeeded to their patrimonies are compelled by this tide of opposition to think and study for themselves. Each man finds himself left face to face with the great hereafter, and his relation to it.

Terrible doctrines are formulated, and press themselves with remorseless vigour upon his understanding—original sin, justification by faith, eternal damnation for even honest error of belief,—doctrines that throw an atmosphere of solemnity, if not gloom, about national thought, in which no fairy mythology can flourish. It is no longer questions of material ease and gain that are of the chief concern; and consequently the fairies and their doings, from their own triviality, fall far into the background, and their place is occupied by a countless horde of remorseless schemers, who are never ceasing in their efforts to drag both body and soul to perdition.

115. But it is in the towns, the centres of interchange of thought, of learning, and of controversy, that this revolution first gathers power; the sparsely populated country-sides are far more impervious to the new ideas, and the country people cling far longer and more tenaciously to the dying religion and its attendant beliefs. The rural districts were but little affected by the Reformation for years after it had triumphed in the towns, and consequently the beliefs of the inhabitants were hardly touched by the struggle that was going on within so short a distance. We find a Reginald Scot, indeed, complaining, half in joke, half in sarcasm, that

Robin Goodfellow has long disappeared from the land;[1] but it is only from the towns that he has fled—towns in which the spirit of the Cartwrights and the Latimers, the Barnhams and the Delabers, is abroad. In the same Cambridge where Scot had been educated, a young student had hanged himself because the shadow of the doctrine of predestination was too terrible for him to live under;[2] and such a place was surely no home for Puck and his merry band. But in the country places, remote from the growl and trembling of this mental earthquake, he still loved to lurk; and even at the very moment when Scot was penning the denial of his existence, he was nestling amongst the woods and flowers of Avonside, and, invisible, whispering in the ear of a certain fair-haired youth there thoughts of no inconsiderable moment. And long time after

that—after the youth had become a man, and had coined those thoughts into words that glitter still; after his monument had been erected in the quiet Stratford churchyard—Puck revelled, harmless and undisturbed, along many a country-side; nay, even to the present day, in some old-world nooks, a faint whispering rumour of him may still be heard.

[Footnote 1: Scot, Introduction.]

[Footnote 2: Foxe, iv. p. 694.]

116. Now, perhaps one of the most distinctive marks of literary genius is a certain receptivity of mind; a capability of receiving impressions from all surrounding circumstance—of extracting from all sources, whether from nature or man, consciously or unconsciously, the material upon which it shall work. For this process to be perfectly accomplished, an entire and enthusiastic sympathy with man and the current ideas of the time is absolutely essential, and in proportion as this sympathy is contracted and partial, so will the work produced be stunted and untrue; and, on the other hand, the more universal and entire it is, the more perfect and vital will be the art. Bearing this in mind, and also the facts that Shakspere's early training was effected in a little country village; that upon the verge of manhood, he came to London, where he

spent his prime in contact with the bustle and friction of busy town life; and that the later years of his life were passed in the quiet retirement of the home of his boyhood—there would be good ground for an argument, *a priori*, even were there none of a more conclusive nature, that his earlier works would be found impregnated with the country fairy-myths with which his youth would come in contact; that the result of the labours of his middle life would show that these earlier reminiscenses had been gradually obliterated by the gloomier influence of ideas that were the result of the struggle of opposed theories that had not then ceased to rage in the towns, and that the diabolic element and questions relating thereto would predominate; and that, finally, his later works, written under the calmer influence of Stratford life, would show a certain return to the fairy-lore of his earlier years.

117. But fortunately we are not left to rely upon any such hypothetical evidence in this matter, however probable it may appear. Although the general reading public cannot be asked to accept as infallible any chronological order of Shakspere's plays that dogmatically asserts a particular sequence, or to investigate the somewhat dry and specialist arguments upon which the conclusions are founded, yet there are certain groupings into periods which areagreed upon as accurate by nearly all critics, and which, without the slightest danger of error, may be asserted to be correct. For instance, it is indisputable that

"Love's Labour's Lost,""The Comedy of Errors,""Romeo and Juliet," and "A Midsummer Night's Dream" are amongst Shakspere's earliest works; that the tragedies of "Julius Caesar,""Hamlet,""Othello,""Macbeth," and "Lear" are the productions of his middle life, between 1600 and 1606; and that "A Winter's Tale" and "The Tempest" are amongst the latest plays which he wrote.[1] Here we have everything that is required to prove the question in hand. At the commencement and at the end of his writings—when a youth fresh from the influence of his country nurture and education, and when a mature man, settling down into the old life again after a long and victorious struggle with the world, with his accumulated store of experience—we find plays which are perfectly saturated with fairy-lore: "The Dream" and

"The Tempest." These are the poles of Shakspere's thought in this respect; and in the centre, imbedded as it were between two layers of material that do not bear any distinctive stamp of their own, but appear rather as a medium for uniting the diverse strata, lie the great tragedies, produced while he was in the very rush and swirl of town life, and reflecting accurately, as we have seen, many of the doubts and speculations that were agitating the minds of men who were ardently searching out truth. It is worth noting too, in passing, that directly Shakspere steps out of his beaten path to depict, in "The Merry Wives of Windsor," the happy country life and manners of his day, he at the same time returns to fairyland again, and brings out the Windsor children trooping to pinch and plague the town-bred, tainted Falstaff.

[Footnote 1: For an elaborate and masterly investigation of the question of the chronological order of the plays, which must be assumed here, see Mr.

Furnivall's Introduction to the Leopold Shakspere.]

118. But this is not by any means all that this subject reveals to us about Shakspere; if it were, the less said about it the better. To look upon "The Tempest" as in its essence merely a return to "The Dream"—the end as the beginning; to believe that his thoughts worked in a weary, unending circle—that the Valley of the Shadow of Death only leads back to the foot of the Hill Difficulty—is intolerable, and not more intolerable than false. Although based upon similar material, the ideas and tendencies of "The Tempest" upon supernaturalism are no more identical with those of "A Midsummer Night's Dream" than the thoughts of Berowne upon things in general are those of Hamlet, or Hamlet's those of Prospero. But before it is possible to point out the nature of this difference, and to show that the change is a natural growth ofthought, not a mere retrogression, a few explanatory remarks are necessary.

There is no more insufficient and misleading view of Shakspere and his work than that which until recently obtained almost universal credence, and is even at the present time somewhat loudly asserted in some quarters; namely, that he was a man of considerable genius, who wrote and got acted some thirty plays more or less, simply for commercial purposes and nothing more; made money thereby, and died leaving a will; and that, beyond this, he and his works are, and must remain, an inexplicable mystery. The critic who holds this view, and finds it equally advantageous to commence a study of Shakspere's work by taking "The Tempest" or "Love's Labour's Lost" as his text, is about as judicious as the botanist who would enlarge upon the structure of the seed-pod without first explaining the preliminary stages of plant growth, or the architect who would dilate upon the most convenient arrangement of chimney-pots before he had discussed the laws of foundation. The plays may be studied separately, and studied so are found beautiful; but taken in an approximate chronological order, like a string of brilliant jewels, each one gains lustre from those that precede and follow it.

119. For no man ever wrote sincerely and earnestly, or indeed ever did any one thing in such a spirit, without leaving some impress upon his work of his mental condition whilst he was doing it; and no such man ever continued his literary labours from the period of youth right through his manhood, without leaving behind him, in more or less legible character, a record of the ripening of his thought upon matters of eternal importance, although they may not be of necessity directly connected with the ostensible subject in hand. Insincere men may ape sentiments they do not really believe in; but in the end they will either be exposed and held up to ridicule, or their work will sink into obscurity.

Sincerity in the expression of genuine thought and feeling alone can stand the test of time. And this is in reality no contradiction to what has just been said as to the necessity of a receptive condition of mind in the production of works of true genius. This capacity of receiving the most delicate objective impressions is, indeed, one essential; but without the cognate power to assimilate this food, and evolve the result that these influences have produced subjectively, it is, worse than useless. The two must co-exist and act and react upon one another. Nor must we be induced to surrender these principles, in the present particular case, on account of the usual fine but vague talk about Shakspere's absolute self-annihilation in favour of the characters that he depicts. It is said that Shakspere so identifies himself with each person in his dramas, that it is impossible to

detect the great master and his thoughts behind this cunningly devised screen. If this means that Shakespere has always a perfect comprehension of his characters, is competent to measure out to each absolute and unerring justice, and is capable of sympathy with even the most repulsive, it will not be disputed for an instant. It is so true, that it is dangerous to take a sentence out of the mouth of any one of his characters and say for certain, "This Shakspere thought," although there are many characters with whom every one must feel that Shakspere identified himself for the time being rather than others. But if it is intended to assert that Shakspere has so eliminated himself from his writings as to make it impossible to trace anywhere the tendencies of his own thought at the time when he was writing, it must be most emphatically denied for the reasons just stated. Freedom from prejudice must be carefully dissociated from lack of interest in the motive that underlies the construction of each play. There is a tone or key-note in each drama that indicates the author's mental condition at the time when it was produced; and if several plays, following each other in brisk succession, all have the same predominant tone, it seems to be past question that Shakspere is incidentally and indirectly uttering his own personal thought and experience.

120. If it be granted, then, that it is possible to follow thus the growth of Shakspere's thought through the medium of his successive works, there is only one small point to be glanced at before attempting to trace this growth in the matter of supernaturalism.

The natural history of the evolution of opinion upon matters which, for want of a more embracing and satisfactory word, we must be content to call "religious," follows a uniform course in the minds of all men, except those "duller than the fat weed that roots itself at ease on Lethe's wharf," who never get beyond the primary stage. This course is separable into three periods. The first is that in which a man accepts unhesitatingly the doctrines which he has received from his spiritual teachers—customary not intellectual, belief. This sits lightly on him; entails no troublesome doubts and questionings; possesses, or appears to possess, formulae to meet all possible emergencies, and consequently brings with it a happiness that is genuine, though superficial. But this customary belief rarely satisfies for long. Contact with the world brings to light other and opposed theories: introspection and independent investigation of the bases of the hereditary faith are commenced; many doctrines that have been hitherto accepted as eternally and indisputably true are found to rest upon but slight foundation, apart from their title to respect on account of age; doubts follow as to the claimto acceptance of the whole system that has been so easily and unhesitatingly swallowed; and the period of scepticism, or no-belief, with its attendant misery, commences—for although Dagon has been but little honoured in the time of his strength, in his downfall he is much regretted. Then comes that long, weary groping after some firm, reliable basis of belief: but heaven and earth appear for the time to conspire against the seeker; an intellectual flood has drowned out the old order of things; not even a mountain peak appears in the wide waste of desolation as assurance of ultimate rest; and in the dark, overhanging firmament no arc of promise is to be seen. But this is a state of mind which, from its very nature, cannot continue for ever: no man could endure it. While it lasts the struggle must be continuous, but somewhere through the cloud lies the sunshine and the land of peace—the final period of intellectual belief. Out of the chaos comes order; ideas that but recently appeared confused, incoherent, and meaningless assume their true perspective. It is found that all the strands of the old conventional faith have not been snapped in the turmoil; and these, re-knit and strengthened with the new and full knowledge of experience and investigation, form the cable that secures that strange holy confidence of belief that can only be gained by a preliminary warfare with doubt—a peace that truly passes all understanding to those who have never battled for it,—as to its foundation, diverse to a miracle in diverse minds, but still, a peace.

121. If this be a true history of the course of development of every mind that is capable of independent thought upon and investigation of such high matters, it follows that Shakspere's soul must have experienced

a similar struggle—for he was a man of like passions with ourselves; indeed, to so acute and sensitive a mind the struggle would be, probably, more prolonged and more agonizing than to many; and it is these three mental conditions—first, of unthinking acceptance of generally received teaching; second, of profound and agitating scepticism; and, thirdly, of belief founded upon reason and experience—that may be naturally expected to be found impressed upon his early, middle, and later works.

122. It is impossible here to do more than indicate some of the evidence that this supposition is correct, for to attempt to investigate the question exhaustively would involve the minute consideration of a majority of the plays. The period of Shakspere's customary or conventional belief is illustrated in "A Midsummer Night's Dream," and to a certain extent also in the "Comedy of Errors." In the former play we find him loyally accepting certain phases of the hereditary Stratford belief in supernaturalism, throwing them into poetical form, and making them beautiful. It has often before been observed, and it is well worthyof observation, that of the three groups of characters in the play, the country folk

—a class whose manner and appearance had most vividly reflected themselves upon the camera of Shakspere's mind—are by far the most lifelike and distinct; the fairies, who had been the companions of his childhood and youth in countless talks in the ingle and ballads in the lanes, come second in prominence and finish; whilst the ostensible heroes and heroines of the piece, the aristocrats of Athens, are colourless and uninteresting as a dumb-show—the real shadows of the play. This is exactly the ratio of impressionability that the three classes would have for the mind of the youthful dramatist. The first is a creation from life, the second from traditionary belief, the third from hearsay. And when it has been said that the fairies are a creation from traditionary belief, a full and accurate description of them has been afforded. They are an embodiment of a popular superstition, and nothing more. They do not conceal any thought of the poet who has created them, nor are they used for any deeper purpose with regard to the other persons of the drama than temporary and objectless annoyance.

Throughout the whole play runs a healthy, thoughtless, honest, almost riotous happiness; no note of difficulty, no shadow of coming doubt being perceptible.

The pert and nimble spirit of mirth is fully awakened; the worst tricks of the intermeddling spirits are mischievous merely, and of only transitory influence, and "the summer still doth tend upon their state," brightening this fairyland with its sunshine and flowers. Man has absolutely no power to govern these supernatural powers, and they have but unimportant influence over him. They can affect his comfort, but they cannot control his fate. But all this is merely an adapting and elaborating of ideas which had been handed down from father to son for many generations. Shakspere's Puck is only the Puck of a hundred ballads reproduced by the hand of a true poet; no original thought upon the connection of the visible with the invisible world is imported into the creation.

All these facts tend to show that when Shakspere wrote "A Midsummer Night's Dream," that is, at the beginning of his career as a dramatic author, he had not broken away from the trammels of the beliefs in which he had been brought up, but accepted them unhesitatingly and joyously.

123. But there is a gradual toning down of this spirit of unbroken content as time wears on. Putting aside the historical plays, in which Shakspere was much more bound down by his subject-matter than in any other species of drama, we find the comedies, in which his room for expression of individual feeling was practically unlimited, gradually losing their unalloyed hilarity, and deepening down into a sadness of thought and expression that sometimes leaves a doubt whether the plays should be classed as comedies at all. Shakspere has been moreand more in contact with the disputes and doubts of the educated men of his time, and seeds have been silently sowing themselves in his heart, which are soon to bring forth a plenteous harvest in the great tragedies of which these semi-comedies, such as "All's Well that Ends Well" and "Measure for Measure," are but the first-fruits.

124. Thus, when next we find Shakspere dealing with questions relating to supernaturalism, the tone is quite different from that taken in his earlier work. He has reached the second period of his thought upon the subject, and this has cast its attendant gloom upon his writings. That he was actually battling with questions current in his time is demonstrated by the way in which, in three consecutive plays, derived from utterly diverse sources, the same question of ghost or devil is agitated, as has before been pointed out. But it is not merely a point of theological dogma which stamps these plays as the product of Shakspere's period of scepticism, but a theory of the influence of supernatural beings upon the whole course of human life. Man is still incapable of influencing these unseen forces, or bending them to his will; but they are now no longer harmless, or incapable of anything but temporary or trivial evil. Puck might lead night wanderers into mischance, and laugh mischievously at the bodily harm that he had caused them; but Puck has now disappeared, and in his stead is found a malignant spirit, who seeks to laugh his fiendish laughter over the soul he has deceived into destruction. Questions arise thick and fast that are easier put than answered. Can it be that evil influences have the upper hand in this world? that, be a man never so honest, never so pure, he may nevertheless become the sport of blind chance or ruthless wickedness? May a Hamlet, patiently struggling after truth and duty, be put upon and abused by the darker powers? May Macbeth, who would fain do right, were not evil so ever present with him, be juggled with and led to destruction by fiends? May an undistinguishing fate sweep away at once the good with the evil—Hamlet with Laertes; Desdemona with Iago; Cordelia with Edmund? And above the turmoil of this reign of terror, is there no word uttered of a Supreme Good guiding and controlling the unloosed ill—no word of encouragement, none of hope? If this be so indeed, that man is but the puppet of malignant spirits, away with this life. It is not worth the living; for what power has man against the fiends? But at this point arises a further question to demand solution: what shall be hereafter? If evil is supreme here, shall it not be so in that undiscovered country,—that life to come? The dreams that may come give him pause, and he either shuffles on, doubting, hesitating, and incapable of decision, or he hurls himself wildly against his fate. In either case his life becomes like to a tale

"Told by an idiot, full of sound and fury, Signifying—nothing!"

125. It is strange to note, too, how the ebb of this wave of scepticism upon questions relating to the immaterial world is only recoil that adds force to a succeeding wave of cynicism with regard to the physical world around.

"Hamlet,""Macbeth," and "Othello" give place to "Lear,""Troilus and Cressida,""Antony and Cleopatra," and "Timon." So true is it that "unfaith in aught is want of faith in all," that in these later plays it would seem that honour, honesty, and justice were virtues not possessed by man or woman; or, if possessed, were only a curse to bring down disgrace and destruction upon the possessor. Contrast the women of these plays with those of the comedies immediately preceding the Hamlet period. In the latter plays we find the heroines, by their sweet womanly guidance and gentle but firm control, triumphantly bringing good out of evil in spite of adverse circumstance.

Beatrice, Rosalind, Viola, Helena, and Isabella are all, not without a tinge of knight-errantry that does not do the least violence to the conception of tender, delicate womanhood, the good geniuses of the little worlds in which their influence is made to be felt. Events must inevitably have gone tragically but for their intervention. But with the advent of the second period all this changes. At first the women, like Brutus' Portia, Ophelia, Desdemona, however noble or sweet in character and well meaning in motive, are incapable of grasping the guiding threads of the events around them and controlling them for good. They have to give way to characters of another kind, who bear the form without the nature of women. Commencing with Lady Macbeth, the conception falls lower and lower, through Goneril and Regan, Cressida, Cleopatra, until in the climax of this utter despair, "Timon," there is no character that it would not be a profanity to call by the name of woman.

126. And just as womanly purity and innocence quail before unwomanly self-assertion and voluptuousness, so manly loyalty and unselfishness give way before unmanly treachery and self-seeking. It is

true that the bad men do not finally triumph, but they triumph over the good with whom they happen to come in contact. In "King Lear," what man shows any virtue who does not receive punishment for the same? Not Gloucester, whose loyal devotion to his king obtains for him a punishment that is only merciful in that it prevents him from further suffering the sight of his beloved master's misery; not Kent, who, faithful in his self-denying service through all manner of obloquy, is left at last with a prayer that he may be allowed to follow Lear to the grave; and beyond these two there is little good to be found. But "Lear" is not by any means the climax. The utter despair of good in man or woman rises higher in "Troilus and Cressida," and reaches its culminating point in "Timon," a fragment only of which is Shakspere's. The pen fell from the tired hand; the worn and distracted brain refused to fulfil the task of depicting the depth to which the poet's estimate of mankind had fallen; and we hardly know whether to rejoice or to regret that the clumsy hand of an inferior writer has screened from our knowledge the full disclosure of the utter and contemptuous cynicism and want of faith with which, for the time being, Shakspere was infected.

127. Before passing on to consider the plays of the third period as evidence of Shakspere's final thought, it will be well to pause and re-read with attention a summing-up of Shakspere's teaching as it has been presented to us by one of the greatest and most earnest teachers of morality of the present day. Every word that Mr. Ruskin writes is so evidently from the depth of his own good heart, and every doctrine that he enunciates so pure in theory and so true in practice, that a difference with him upon the final teaching of Shakspere's work cannot be too cautiously expressed. But the estimate of this which he has given in the third Lecture of "Sesame and Lilies"[1] is so painful, if regarded as Shakspere's latest and most mature opinion, that everybody, even Mr. Ruskin himself, would be glad to modify its gloom with a few rays of hope, if it were possible to do so.

"What then," says Mr. Ruskin, "is the message to us of our own poet and searcher of hearts, after fifteen hundred years of Christian faith have been numbered over the graves of men? Are his words more cheerful than the heathen's (Homer)? is his hope more near, his trust more sure, his reading of fate more happy? Ah no! He differs from the heathen poet chiefly in this, that he recognizes for deliverance no gods nigh at hand, and that, by petty chance, by momentary folly, by broken message, by fool's tyranny, or traitor's snare, the strongest and most righteous are brought to their ruin, and perish without word of hope. He, indeed, as part of his rendering of character, ascribes the power and modesty of habitual devotion to the gentle and the just. The death-bed of Katharine is bright with visions of angels; and the great soldier-king, standing by his few dead, acknowledges the presence of the hand that can save alike by many or by few. But observe that from those who with deepest spirit meditate, and with deepest passion mourn, there are no such words as these; nor in their hearts are any such consolations. Instead of the perpetual sense of the helpful presence of the Deity, which, through all heathen tradition, is the source of heroic strength, in battle, in exile, and in the valley of the shadow of death, we find only in the great Christian poet the consciousness of a moral law, throughwhich 'the gods are just, and of our pleasant vices make instruments to scourge us;' and of the resolved arbitration of the destinies, that conclude into precision of doom what we feebly and blindly began; and force us, when our indiscretion serves us, and our deepest plots do pall, to the confession that 'there's a divinity that shapes our ends, rough-hew them how we will.'"[2]

[Footnote 1: 3rd edition, § 115.]

[Footnote 2: Mr. Ruskin has analyzed "The Tempest," in "Munera Pulveris," § 124, et seqq., but from another point of view.]

128. Now, it is perfectly clear that this criticism was written with two or three plays, all belonging to one period, very conspicuously before the mind. Of the illustrative exceptions that are made to the general rule, one is derived from a play which Shakspere wrote at a very early date, and the other from a scene which he almost certainly never wrote at all; the whole of the rest of the passage quoted is founded upon "Hamlet,""Macbeth,""Othello," and "Lear"—that is, upon the earlier productions of what we must call Shakspere's sceptical period.

But these plays represent an essentially transient state of thought. Shakspere was to learn and to teach that those who most deeply meditate and most passionately mourn are not the men of noblest or most influential character—that such may command our sympathy, but hardly our respect or admiration. Still less did Shakspere finally assert, although for a time he believed, that a blind destiny concludes into precision what we feebly and blindly begin. Far otherwise and nobler was his conception of man and his mission, and the unseen powers and their influences, in the third and final stage of his thought.

129. Had Shakspere lived longer, he would doubtless have left us a series of plays filled with the bright and reassuring tenderness and confidence of this third period, as long and as brilliant in execution as those of the second period. But as it is we are in possession of quite enough material to enable us to form accurate conclusions upon the state of his final thought. It is upon "The Tempest" that we must in the main rely for an exposition of this; for though the other plays and fragments fully exhibit the restoration of his faith in man and woman, which was a necessary concurrence with his return from scepticism, yet it is in "The Tempest" that he brings himself as nearly face to face as dramatic possibilities would allow him with circumstances that admit of the indirect expression of such thought. It is fortunate, too, for the purpose of comparing Shakspere's earliest and latest opinions, that the characters of "The Tempest" are divisibleinto the same groups as those of "The Dream." The gross *canaille* are represented, but now no longer the most accurate in colour and most absorbing in interest of the characters of the play, or unessential to the evolution of the plot.

They have a distinct importance in the movement of the piece, and represent the unintelligent, material resistance to the work of regeneration that Prospero seeks to carry out, and which must be controlled by him, just as Sebastian and Antonio form the intelligent, designing resistance. The spirit world is there too, but they, like the former class, have no independent plot of their own, and no independent operation against mankind; they only represent the invisible forces over which Prospero must assert control if he would insure success for his schemes. Ariel is, perhaps, one of the most extraordinary of all Shakspere's creations. He is, indeed, formed upon a basis half fairy, half devil, because it was only through the current notions upon demonology that Shakspere could speak his ideas. But he certainly is not a fairy in the sense that Puck is a fairy; and he is very far indeed from bearing even a slight resemblance to the familiars whom the magicians of the time professed to call from the vasty deep. He is indeed but air, as Prospero says—the embodiment of an idea, the representative of those invisible forces which operate as factors in the shaping of events which, ignored, may prove resistant or fatal, but, properly controlled and guided, work for good.

[1] Lastly, there are the heroes and heroine of the play, now no longer shadows, but the centres of interest and admiration, and assuming their due position and prominence.

[Footnote 1: It is difficult to accept Mr. Ruskin's view of Ariel as "the spirit of generous and free-hearted service" (Mun. Pul. § 124); he is throughout the play the more-than-half-unwilling agent of Prospero.]

130. It is probable, therefore, that it is not merely a student's fancy that in Prospero's storm-girt, spirit-haunted island can be seen Shakspere's final and matured image of the mighty world. If this be so, how far more bright and hopeful it is than the verdict which Mr. Ruskin finds Shakspere to have returned.

Man is no longer "a pipe for fortune's fingers to sound what stop she please."

The evil elements still exist in the world, and are numerous and formidable; but man, by nobleness of life and word, by patience and self-mastery, can master them, bring them into subjection, and make them tend to eventual good. Caliban, the gross, sensual, earthly element— though somewhat raised—would run riot, and is therefore compelled to menial service. The brute force of Stephano and Trinculo is vanquished by mental superiority. Even the supermundane spirits, now no longer thirsting for the destruction of body and soul, are bound down to

the work of carrying out the decrees of truth and justice. Man is no longer the plaything, but the master of his fate; and he, seeing now the possible triumph of good over evil, and his duty to do his best in aid of this triumph, has no more fear of the dreams—the something after death. Our little life is still rounded by a sleep, but the thought which terrifies Hamlet has no power to affright Prospero.

The hereafter is still a mystery, it is true; he has tried to see into it, and has found it impenetrable. But revelation has come like an angel, with peace upon its wings, in another and an unexpected way. Duty lies here, in and around him in this world. Here he can right wrong, succour the weak, abase the proud, do something to make the world better than he found it; and in the performance of this he finds a holier calm than the vain strivings after the unknowable could ever afford. Let him work while it is day, for "the night cometh, when no man can work."

131. It is not a piece of pure sentimentality that sees in Prospero a type of Shakspere in his final stage of thought. It is a type altogether as it should be; and it is pleasing to think of him, in the full maturity of his manhood, wrapping his seer's cloak about him, and, while waiting calmly the unfolding of the mystery which he has sought in vain to solve, watching with noble benevolence the gradual working out of truth, order, and justice. It is pleasing to think of him as speaking to the world the great Christian doctrine so universally overlooked by Christians, that the only remedy for sin demanded by eternal justice "is nothing but heart's sorrow, and a clear life ensuing"—a speech which, though uttered by Ariel, is spoken by Prospero, who himself beautifully iterates part of the doctrine when he says—

"The rarer action is

In virtue than in vengeance: they being penitent, The sole drift of my purpose doth extend

Not a frown further."[1]

It is pleasant to dwell upon his sympathy with Ferdinand and Miranda—for the love of man and woman is pure and holy in this regenerate world: no more of Troilus and Cressida—upon his patient waiting for the evolution of his schemes; upon his faith in their ultimate success; and, above all, upon the majestic and unaffected reverence that appears indirectly in every line—"reverence," to adapt the words of the great teacher whose opinion about Shakspere has been perhaps too rashly questioned, "for what is pure and bright in youth; for what is true and tried in age; for all that is gracious among the living, great among the dead, and

marvellous in the Powers that cannot die."

[Footnote 1: V. 1. 27.]

***END

CPSIA information can be obtained
at www.ICGtesting.com
Printed in the USA
BVHW090921170922
647223BV00019B/1512

9 781006 028526